Warship Design Histories

Fletcher-Class Destroyers

Warship Design Histories

Naval Institute Press
Annapolis, Maryland

FLETCHER-CLASS DESTROYERS

By Alan Raven

Library of Congress Cataloging-in-Publication Data
Raven, Alan.
  Fletcher-class destroyers.
  1. Destroyers (Warships)—United States. I. Title.
V825.3.R38 1986   359.3′254′0973   86-12559
ISBN 0-87021-147-1

Printed in the United States of America

Contents

Acknowledgments

A number of individuals gave freely and generously of their time and materials, and without their help this volume would be poorer: L. Sowinsky of the Intrepid Air and Sea Space Museum in New York City; A.D. Baker III of Virginia; N. Friedman of New York; D. Shaddell of New Jersey; R. Morales of New Jersey; E. Arroyo of Connecticut; A. Charles and P. Walsh of the National Park Service in Boston, Massachusetts; J. Boulware, ex-commanding officer of the *Heywood L. Edwards*; W. Voss of Virginia; R. Champler of Massachusetts; and C. Evers of Connecticut; and last but not least, special thanks to my wife.

Warship Design Histories

Fletcher-Class Destroyers

Introduction

Although American warships of the World War II period have been described extensively over the years, these descriptions have tended to emphasize the operational aspect, with a marked lack of actual ship descriptions. It was felt, therefore, that the time was right to take the most numerous and most famous destroyer class of the war and attempt to present as complete a visual coverage as space and available material allowed. This would then enable the reader to understand, in a way not possible before, just what these ships looked like and how they were fitted out in service.

With 175 ships in the class, it is impossible to describe every one, but the author has attempted to cover a substantial number, along with the many variations in their configuration and equipment.

Drawings have been used whenever possible, in line with available data, and should be viewed in conjunction with the large number of photos that have been included, so that if a certain layout or piece of equipment is not shown in drawing form, the chances are that it will appear in a photo.

A high percentage of the drawings derive from official material that has come from a variety of sources. The sketch designs came from Department of Construction and Repair documents; the general arrangement ship plans from booklet plans, as did a large number of working drawings, while various equipment views originated in manuals and textbooks. In addition, many drawings were prepared using specially taken photographs so as to give unique angles.

For the model maker, material has been included that describes some of the camouflage schemes worn by the class, as well as a selection of ship's emblems.

A special effort was made to present a comprehensive amount of new material in a clear and attractive manner, and although there are the inevitable gaps in the coverage (mainly because of space restrictions) it is hoped that the reader will allow for this.

Of all the destroyer classes to serve in World War II, there is no doubt that the ships of the *Fletcher* class are the most famous and well known. Described by one famous commander as the "perfect fighting destroyer," 175 were built in a two-and-one-half-year period, a stunning example of World War II warship standardization and mass production.

Design

Ironically, the *Fletcher* type came into being because of a desire to produce a *smaller* destroyer than the preceding classes, i.e., the *Benson* and *Sims* groups. Concern had been expressed, especially with the *Benson*s, that their large size had begun to make them targets in their own right. In addition, the previously much-discussed debate about the proper balance between gun and torpedo armament was raised again in the fall of 1939, and it soon became obvious that getting a ship of smaller displacement was not a practical proposition if the required torpedo and gun armament were to be maintained. In addition, there was a growing need, soon to be reinforced by British combat experience, for ASW and AA weapons and equipment.

Destroyers had always been fast ships, but in 1939 and 1940, the navy had on the drawing boards carriers and battleships that would be able to make 33 knots, and the destroyers would therefore have to have a margin of speed over these ships of at least 5 knots. To obtain 38 knots with the new ships would mean that the previous *Benson*-class design could not be used.

In addition to the above concern, the *Sims* class, which was just coming into service, was showing serious construction deficiencies. The ships proved badly overweight as completed and of too lightweight a construction, with every vessel having to undergo an extensive Navy Yard refit upon delivery from the builders before being deemed fit for service. This would mean that any new design would have to be more strongly constructed, resulting in a greater displacement for the same military characteristics.

In mid-October 1939, the General Board stated the initial characteristics.* These were:

- Displacement 1,600 tons (maximum)
- Armament four 5-inch guns (maximum)
  two quintuple torpedo tubes
  twenty-eight depth charges
  four 0.5-inch machine guns
- General to be of rugged construction
  so as to be able to maintain
  high speed in rough
  weather†
- Endurance 6,500 NM at 12 knots (four
  months out of dock)

In response, three designs were submitted:

- A *Benson*—modified in respect to depth-charge arrangements
- A vessel with four 5-inch guns
- A vessel with a combination of twin- and single-mounted 5-inch guns.

Although these designs must have been discussed by the board in some detail, there is unfortunately no mention of the first and second sketches—only a rejection of the third on the grounds that a hit on one of the twin mountings would reduce the available firepower by an unacceptable percentage. Whatever the reasons for the rejections, a further set of sketches was submitted in November 1939. Most surprisingly, all six of these new designs were based upon the *Sims* hull (an unsuccessful design), except that one foot was added to the beam for a greater range of stability in four of the schemes. In two of

---

* The General Board was established during the Spanish American War. It was initially concerned with long-range planning, but by 1908 had also become responsible for the general characteristics of U. S. warships. From 1920 to 1942 it decided much of U.S. naval policy and then gradually lost influence until it was disbanded in 1951, it's work being taken over by the office of the Chief of Naval Operations.

† Author's note: What speed in what sea state is not known. In addition, no top-speed requirement was stated.

Table A. Schemes 1–6

	1	2	3	4	5	6
Displacement						
(Standard)	1,720	1,690	1,685	1,685	1,695	1,725
(Trial)	2,163	2,131	2,125	2,121	2,134	2,166
Length (W/L)			341'			
Length (O/A)			348'			
Beam	37'	37'	36'	36'	37'	37'
Speed	36.5 knots	36.5 knots	36.5 knots	36.5 knots	36.5 knots	36.5 knots
Armament				1 twin	1 twin	1 twin
5" guns	5 singles	4 singles	2 twins	2 singles	2 singles	3 singles
0.5" machine guns			4 single mounts			
Protection	None	None	None	None	None	None
Endurance (nautical miles)			6,500			

Table B. Schemes 1ᴬ–1ᶠ

	1ᴬ	1ᴮ	1ᶜ	1ᴰ	1ᴱ	1ᶠ
Displacement						
(standard)	1,735	1,735	1,754	1,772	1,745	1,796
(trial)	2,180	2,180	2,199	2,218	2,191	2,241
Beam	37'	37'6"	37'6"	37'6"	38'	38'
Protection (STS)*						
Machinery	20 lbs	None	20 lbs	30 lbs	None	30 lbs
Bridge	None	20 lbs	20 lbs	None	30 lbs	30 lbs

*Special Treatment Steel

these, there were four or five 5-inch guns in single mounts, while the remaining schemes showed a combination of twin and single 5-inch mountings. The twin-mount designs allowed for a reduction in superstructure and consequently in silhouette. As an additional feature, aluminum was to be extensively used to reduce topweight. With the new, more efficient machinery fitted, the endurance would rise to 6,500 NM at 15 knots. (See table A.)

In the same period that designs 1ᴬ–1ᶠ were being presented, an additional design was offered for examination—one that appears to have been conceived without a General Board request. Design 7 called for:

- Displacement (standard)   1,685
- Displacement (trial)   2,126
- Beam   37'0"
- Armament—5-inch guns   2 singles forward
  2 singles aft
- Protection   none

All the designs presented were compromises, and none achieved the new desired top speed of 38 knots, nor did they stay within the 1,600-ton desired maximum displacement, coming out at around 1,700 tons.

The designs were criticized by the Board as being larger than desired and as having no apparent

November 1939 Sketch for Proposed
1941 Program Destroyer Design
Scheme 1
1709 Tons
5 5" Single Guns
2 Quintuple Torpedo Tubes

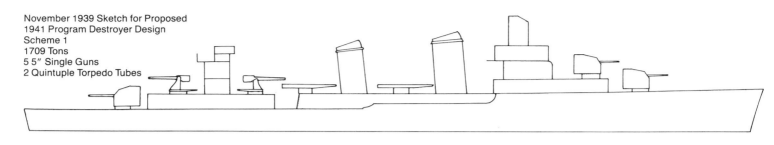

November 1939 Sketch for Proposed
1941 Program Destroyer Design
Scheme 2
1682 Tons
4 5" Single Guns
2 Quintuple Torpedo Tubes

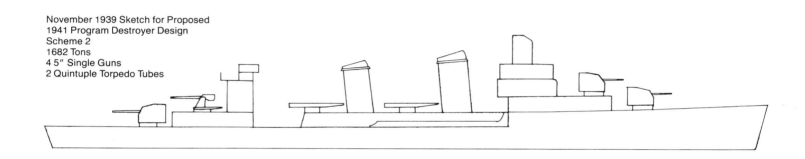

November 1939 Sketch for Proposed
1941 Program Destroyer Design
Scheme 3
1678 Tons
2 Twin 5" Mounts

TWIN MOUNTING

TWIN MOUNTING

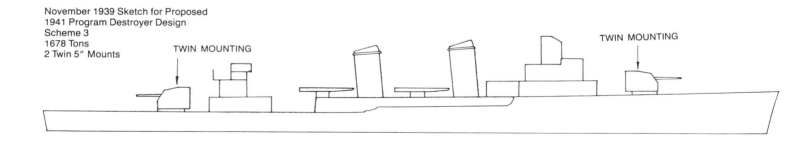

November 1939 Sketch for Proposed
1941 Program Destroyer Design
Scheme 4
1675 Tons
2 Twin 5" Mounts
1 Single 5" Mount
2 Quintuple Torpedo Tubes

TWIN MOUNTING

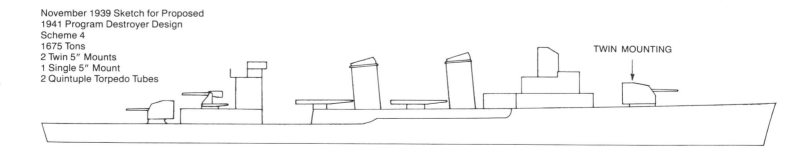

advantages in armament over previous classes, although the designers explained that much of the weight had gone into a stronger hull and natural growth.

Of schemes 1–6, scheme 1 was chosen as the basis for six more designs that were similar, except that they allowed for protection. (See table B.)

The greatest difference from the other schemes was that this design employed flush-deck construction. With this feature, considerable weight would be saved without sacrificing structural strength.

During this time, there was a continuing debate over the number and arrangement of torpedoes and guns, with AA and ASW weaponry playing second fiddle (the war in Europe had yet to make its presence felt).

By the end of November, four more designs of varying characteristics were presented to the Gen-eral Board, all being flush-decked and over 1,700 tons displacement. (See table C.)

Table C. Schemes 7ᴬ–10 (FLUSH-DECKED)

	7A	8	9	10
Displacement				
(standard)	1,745	1,820	1,898	2,000
(trial)	2,200	2,291	2,379	2,500
Length W/L	345'	355'	369'	362'
Length O/A	382'	362'	276'	369'
Beam	37'6"	38'	38'6"	38'9"
Armament				
5" guns on				
single mounts	five	five	four	five
Protection	none	none	30 lbs STS bridge & machinery sides	20 lbs STS bridge & machinery sides

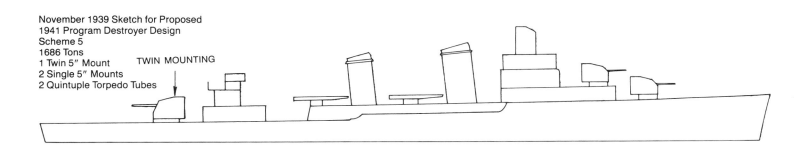

November 1939 Sketch for Proposed
1941 Program Destroyer Design
Scheme 5
1686 Tons
1 Twin 5" Mount
2 Single 5" Mounts
2 Quintuple Torpedo Tubes

TWIN MOUNTING

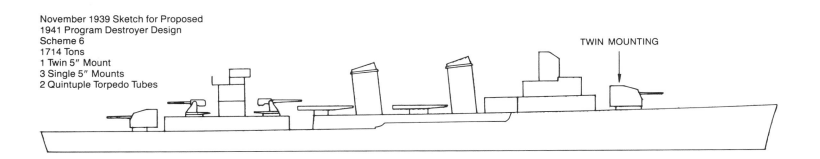

November 1939 Sketch for Proposed
1941 Program Destroyer Design
Scheme 6
1714 Tons
1 Twin 5" Mount
3 Single 5" Mounts
2 Quintuple Torpedo Tubes

TWIN MOUNTING

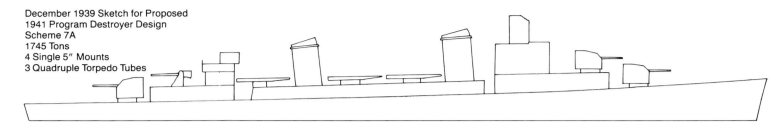

December 1939 Sketch for Proposed
1941 Program Destroyer Design
Scheme 7A
1745 Tons
4 Single 5" Mounts
3 Quadruple Torpedo Tubes

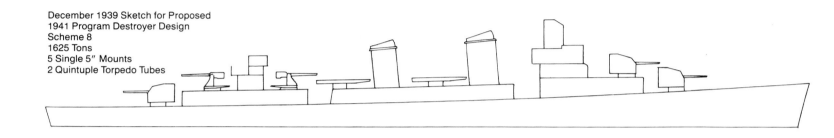

December 1939 Sketch for Proposed
1941 Program Destroyer Design
Scheme 8
1625 Tons
5 Single 5" Mounts
2 Quintuple Torpedo Tubes

Of these four, the last design was up to 2,000 tons and a 60,000 SHP plant, and if lengthened to 369 feet, could achieve 38 knots. As in innumerable other cases of requirements, the governing bodies (in this case the General Board) had priced themselves out of the 1,600-ton-displacement market by asking for too much, without being willing to pay the price. In these later schemes, protection for machinery and fire control had been requested in the light of recent British experience, and this had further added to the displacement.

At some time in late 1939, probably during the discussion period of the November designs, the navy came to realize that with the formal withdrawal by the British from the naval treaties, the Americans were free to build any size of ship desired, regardless of type. Consequently, by early January 1940 four more designs were on the table, designs that had five 5-inch guns, the fitting of the quadruple 1.1-inch mountings for close range AA, and STS protection. (See table D.)

Table D. Schemes 10b–10e

	10b	10c	10d	10e
Displacement				
(standard)	2,017	2,036	2,570	2,082
(trial)	2,510	2,529	2,570	2,585
Length (W/L)	365'	365'	365'	369'
Speed (knots)	38.32	38.15	37.75	38.00
SHP		60,000		
Armament				
5 " guns		5 single mounts		
quad 1.1" mount		one		
0.5" machine guns		4 single mounts		
torpedo tubes		2 quintuple mounts		
Protection (30 lbs STS)	on sides & deck	on sides	on sides & deck	on sides & deck

Out of the many designs submitted and discussed, a final choice was made in January 1940 by the General Board, and was approved by the Secretary of the Navy on the 27th of the month. It had the following features:

- Armament   five 5″ single mountings
  one quadruple 1.1″ machine cannon
  four 0.5″ machine guns
  twenty-eight depth charges
  two quintuple 21″ torpedo tubes
- Protection   30/20 lb STS for sides and deck of machinery and fire control

Construction

With the design now more or less settled, orders were placed by mid-1940 for no less than twenty-four ships, well before the beginning of Fiscal Year 41, and by the end of 1940 almost 100 were on order. To cope with this huge increase, which was, in effect, a war emergency program begun in peacetime, additional shipbuilding facilities had to be found. Those chosen were at San Pedro and Long Beach, California, Chickasaw, Alabama, Orange, Texas, and Seattle, Washington.

With the entry of America into the war in December 1941, repeat orders for *Fletcher*s were placed, bringing the total to 175.

At the end of 1941 and in early 1942, there was a revision in the AA armament of the *Fletcher*s. The approval had been for a quadruple 1.1-inch cannon and four single 0.5-inch machine guns, but the British experience had demonstrated just how out-of-date those weapons were. At the same time, however, there appeared on the scene two more efficient replacements—the 40-mm Bofors gun developed before the war by the Dutch, and the 20-mm Swiss Oerlikon.

The British had already had experience with the 20- and 40-mm types on warships, and had found them to be far superior to the 0.5-inch machine gun, which was similar in some respects to the 1.1-inch. Consequently, it was decided to fit the new ships with one twin 40-mm Bofors in the after structure between Nos. 3 and 4 5-inch guns, in lieu of the 1.1-inch mount, and to replace the 0.5-inch machine

gun with single 20-mm mountings. This could be done without any significant increase in displacement; as an alternative, and if some of the STS protection was removed, then two twin Bofors could be installed.

The first ship of the *Fletcher* class to commission was the *Nicholas*, on 4 June 1942. On trials she reached a top speed of 37 knots instead of the expected 38, and at the very substantial size of 2,589 tons displacement, brought about by the many wartime additions. The results of the *Nicholas* trials indicated that a maximum continuous sea speed of around 32/33 knots could be expected, no more than those of previous classes.

The first ships to complete—the *Nicholas*, *Fletcher*, and *O'Bannon*—still carried the 1.1-inch cannon, installed in the after structure between Nos. 3 and 4 5-inch guns. Six 20-mm were also fitted, two in the front of the bridge, and two in the waist, port and starboard. After running trials and working up, the 1.1-inch mount was removed and replaced by a twin 40-mm Bofors.

Some ships, including the *LaVallette*, were delivered with provision for one twin 40-mm Bofors and six single 20 mm, but *joined the fleet* with two twin Bofors and four single 20 mm. In almost every instance, vessels completing in 1942 were delivered from the builders without radar, and in many cases without the Bofors and only a partial 20-mm battery. In this period, the ships were taken in hand by a navy yard to undergo final fitting out of radar and weaponry. In several instances, the first Bofors installations were unaccompanied by the associated MK 51 director, with the result that many vessels had to go back to the yard for a second visit when this equipment was ready. The end result of this delay was that the first *Fletcher* did not arrive on station in the Pacific until well into the fall of 1942, even though the first deliveries occurred in June. This was to be regretted, as their appearance in the early part of the Guadalcanal Campaign would have helped considerably.

In terms of ASW capability, they were well fitted out for fleet destroyers, having two depth-charge tracks at the stern, each holding eight depth charges, and three "K"-gun throwers that were located abreast the aft deckhouse port and starboard, with four spare charges to each thrower.

They all entered operational service with a complete radar outfit, consisting in 1942 of an SC air-search set, and SG surface-search set with an antenna on a platform high up on the mast, and the MK 37 fire-control director carrying the antenna for the MK 4 fire-control radar upon its roof. Upon entering service in the latter half of 1942, these ships could easily have laid claim to being the best-equipped destroyers in the fleet.

Wartime Modifications

In the spring and summer of 1942, the actions at Coral Sea and Midway had demonstrated firsthand the desperate need for a greatly enhanced AA capability, and the early phases of the Guadalcanal Campaign reinforced this belief. The result (in the *Fletchers*) was an upgrading of the AA outfit. The first measure was an interim arrangement whereby a centerline platform was floated out from the bridge face. This contained a single 20 mm, and usually another single 20 mm was fitted centerline at the forward end of the pilothouse roof. This made a total of eight single 20 mm and two twin Bofors.

These additions began in the last weeks of 1942 and the first weeks of 1943, mostly in completing ships but also in some of those earlier vessels that were having battle damage repaired.

The inevitable wartime growth in weight occasioned a revision of the design in 1942, the main feature of which was to reduce the topweight problem that was becoming acute. This condition was further aggravated by the shortage of aluminum, which meant that mild steel of much greater weight had to be used for the superstructure instead. A ship with an all-steel superstructure was believed to be about 50 tons heavier than one with aluminum.

The remedies taken were to lower the director by six feet, effect a reduction in the STS protection, and reduce the height of the aft superstructure (the last measure had already been carried out in a great majority of the earlier vessels). Another change was the squaring off of the rounded face of the bridge. This saved weight and was easier to produce. During the early months of the war, there had been many complaints from sea that during air attacks, the closed-in, rounded bridge with platform wings did not allow the commander to see all that was happening, especially when the action was occurring port and starboard at the same time, or when the action rapidly moved from one side to the other. Ideally, the solution would have been an open bridge, but this was not possible without a complete redesign and with subsequent loss of building time; the remedy was to run the side platforms completely around the face of the bridge. This could only be done in vessels with square bridges, because in those with round bridges, the bridge projected out too far to accommodate such a feature along with the centerline 20-mm mount already there. The penalty for adopting the square and slightly shortened bridge and reduced height director was the inability to install a 20 mm upon the pilothouse roof. Thus, when the earliest square-bridge vessels appeared in the early spring of 1943, their close-range armament usually consisted of two twin Bofors aft, four 20 mm in the waist, and only three 20 mm around the bridge, for a total of seven 20 mm. Along with these AA additions, completing vessels began to receive an SC-2 air-search radar instead of the older SC set. SC-2 was a much improved set in every way, but due to the larger antenna, there was an unfortunate increase in topweight.

By mid-1943, the AA battery had increased again by the addition of another twin Bofors and three single 20-mm mounts. The Bofors on the fantail was removed, and two twins were placed amidships, one port, one starboard abreast the aft funnel. The moving of the aft Bofors freed space for a pair of depth-

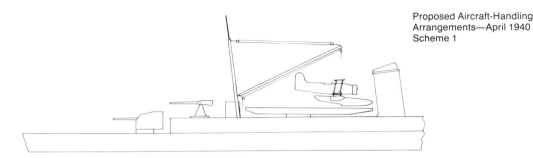

Proposed Aircraft-Handling
Arrangements—April 1940
Scheme 1

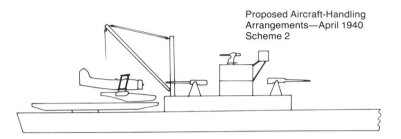

Proposed Aircraft-Handling
Arrangements—April 1940
Scheme 2

charge stowage tracks alongside the dropping tracks.

The positioning of the midships Bofors made it necessary to move the torpedo crane, which was loaced by the aft funnel, to a new location abreast the fore funnel. As this could obviously not serve the aft set of torpedo tubes, an extra crane, one that could telescope down to almost deck level, was installed at the aft end of the midship deckhouse.

Another difference among many *Fletcher*s completing during 1943 from those delivered in 1942 was the fitting of the MK 49 director in lieu of the MK 51 to control the Bofors guns. These directors can easily be distinguished from the MK 51 in that the former was contained within a small turret-like structure.

In the calendar year 1940 *Fletcher* program, there was a requirement that six ships be fitted to operate aircraft to provide gun spotting for the 5-inch guns during bombardment duties, and for general scouting duties when destroyers might be operating without the support of heavier units that also would provide aircraft. This idea was not without considerable opposition, but it was pushed, with the result that six *Fletcher*s were built with arrangements to accommodate a single Kingfisher aircraft. The price for this arrangement was the loss of the No. 3 5-inch gun as well as the superstructure and Bofors mount between the Nos. 3 and 4 5-inch guns.

Of the six, only three actually received tha catapult and aircraft. These were the *Pringle*, *Stevens*, and *Halford*. The operation of aircraft from these ships did not prove successful, and after only a few short months of operations in 1943, the installations were removed. Although the No. 3 5-inch gun, which in each case had been retained in storage, was fitted upon removal of the catapult, the three ships operated for some months without the deckhouse between the No. 3 and 4 guns, and as an interim measure, two single 20-mm mountings were installed in this area.

One of the great deficiencies in destroyers during the first two years of the Pacific war was their lack of effective close-range AA on forward bearings. The problem was exacerbated when attacking aircraft began to weave port to starboard when approaching. The fitting of one or two 20-mm guns on the centerline by the bridge only partially cured this problem; therefore, in June 1943 it was announced that the two forward 20 mm would be replaced by two twin 40-mm Bofors. Partial compensation for this extra weight was accomplished by removing the twin Bofors from the fantail on ships that still carried only two twin Bofors mounts. The platforms that had carried the 20 mm had to be enlarged to allow space for the 40-mm Bofors. In the same month that the order was put out, ships began to appear with the new configuration, with the round- and square-bridge types having five twin Bofors and seven single 20-mm mounts.

CIC

By mid-1942, there was an obvious need for a special area in ships of destroyer size and above, where all information could be sent and collated and subsequent decisions made and orders given. The Combat Information Center (CIC) was an inevitable development born out of the need to coordinate and clarify the high increase in radio traffic between ships, and ships and aircraft, and to maintain knowledge of the tactical disposition of both by radar.

The first CICs began appearing in a handful of *Fletchers*, and could sometimes be identified externally by the greater number of short-wave radio antennas hung from the masts and yardarms. They were installed below the bridge at main-deck level and created congestion below decks, in vessels that were already overcrowded.

Around this time other changes became apparent. The MK 4 radar was being replaced by the MK 12/22 radar, and the 20 mm received the MK 14 computing gunsight. These wartime changes, bringing more additions than deletions, resulted in a gradual but steady overall increase in displacement. Top speed also delined. A late war *Fletcher* could usually only make about 32 or 33 knots, and of course the endurance dropped considerably.

Radar Pickets

With the installation of CICs and the increased communications outfit, 1943 saw the first destroyer to be used in a new role, that of radar picket. The picket's role was to steam ahead of the main force by many miles and in doing so provide advance warning to the fleet. The first destroyer in the navy to be used in this manner was the *Trathen* (DD 530) during the invasion of the Baker and Howland Islands in 1943, and she performed successfully. By the end of the year the picket role was combined with fighter direction for the first time in the *Kimberley* (DD 521).

As more ships were fitted out with CICs, their role naturally expanded, so that by the end of 1944, it was common for one destroyer from each division to act as the fighter-direction ship. Although the roles of picket and fighter direction were closely linked, the picket did not always serve simultaneously as the directing vessel.

The latter part of 1944 found the Japanese employing airborne radar on a substantial scale, with the result that beginning in September 1944 the U.S. Navy began to install, mainly on the *Fletchers*, radar intercept equipment and jamming gear.

The very first installations were made at forward bases, the antennas being attached to the foremast just below the yardarm. This arrangement appears to have been unsatisfactory because shortly afterwards, ships outfitted in the States appeared carrying a short mainmast dedicated to these types of antennas. This probably was due to the increasing number of antennas needed to cover greater frequencies and because at very short wavelengths, other nearby aerials, such as the several short-wave radio antennas fitted to the foremast, would cause ghosting and interfere with reception.

Additional intercept antennas were usually fitted on the sides of the stacks near the top, projecting from the bridge face, while the direction-finding antennas, contained in small radomes, were attached to the mainmast, as were the jamming antennas and the balance of the intercept antennas.

The duties of the typical late-1944 *Fletcher* were as follows:

- To support the fleet against surface attack
- To support the fleet against air attack
- To support the fleet against submarine attack

- To provide shore bombardment for landings and to support troops already established ashore
- To act as radar picket to provide early warning of impending air attacks
- To act as a fighter-direction unit
- To conduct electronic countermeausres (ECM) against radar-supported enemy aircraft attacks

To the above list was added one more requirement—to defend itself against the guided missile, the kamikaze. This deadly weapon made its appearance in the battle of the Philippines in the fall of 1944, and the effects were immediate and devastating. When kamikazes were first used, their main targets were the capital ships, not the destroyers. After the Battle of Leyte Gulf, there was a relative lull in kamikaze attacks until the landings at Okinawa, and it was here that the destroyers, while serving as radar pickets around the island, started to blunt the edge of the Japanese air attacks. Such was the sustained intensity of these attacks that thirteen destroyers were sunk and eighty-eight were damaged, some of the latter so badly that they were declared to be not worth repairing. Of these destroyers, the great majority were *Fletcher*s, and even though almost all of the latter had an AA battery of five Bofors and seven single 20 mm, coupled with the support of perhaps one or two landing craft, this was simply not enough in many cases to avoid being hit by the kamikazes. Some took many hits and survived, while others took only a few and sank.

The cry was immediate and loud, "Give us more AA guns." The only way of achieving this was to remove equivalent topweight, in the form of the forward set of torpedo tubes, thus permitting the installation of two quadruple Bofors mountings and the fitting of the MK 35 radar to give a supposed greater degree of accuracy. The main-deck support house for the quad Bofors was moved several feet forward in order to allow the remaining after torpedo-tube mount a greater arc of fire. As an additional enhancement, the seven single 20 mm were removed and replaced by six twin 20-mm mountings.

When the war was over, there was no need for large fleets of destroyers, and by this time the *Fletcher* was not the new type it had been in 1942 and 1943. It had been superseded by the larger and newer *Sumner*s and *Gearing*s, which had more armament and internal space in which to place the growing amount of "black box" equipment.

It is useful to look over the *Fletcher*s as a class and their performance in wartime. In many ways there is no doubt that they were superior to all the earlier classes. They had greater survivability, due to the installation of unit machinery. (Of the preceding classes, only the *Benson*s had this feature.) They introduced high steam pressures, which gave a high top speed in actual war conditions and increased endurance. The option of the flush deck guaranteed a strong hull for less weight than that of a high-forecastle destroyer, and they had a reserve of stability to allow a continued number of weight additions, some of them being very high up.

On the debit side, the flush deck, when coupled with all the weight additions, drove displacement up and freeboard down, so that in heavy weather the *Fletcher*s were very wet, much more so than any of the earlier classes built between the wars. They were also probably the worst destroyers with respect to maneuverability, to the extent that the succeeding *Sumner* and *Gearing* classes introduced twin rudders into destroyer service. The severe problems with many of the preceding classes, especially the *Bagley*s and the *Sims*, were that the ships had been constructed on a far too flimsy basis. For the *Fletcher*s, that meant a turn-away from ultra-lightweight construction to something more substantial, a decision that paid handsome dividends throughout the war and well beyond. With many of the earlier classes, it had been forgotten that the ship type qualities must come first, not the amount of guns she had or how fast she would go on a given displacement.

It is interesting to note that in the design stage and upon first entry into service in mid-1942, the class was often compared unfavorably with the earlier classes in respect to armament and displacement or ship size, yet it was the *Fletcher*s that without doubt proved to be the most successful American destroyers of World War II, and this is because their design, compared to others, was fairly conservative. It therefore allowed a greater margin for error. Fortunately, the supporting aspects of machinery, armament, sensors, and quality of workmanship were good, and it should be no surprise that they turned out as well as they did. In many aspects, all of the previous classes provided the base of a pyramid of experience upon which the *Fletcher*s eventually formed the peak, and it can be argued that they were the *first* American destroyers to "get it right," in that hull, plant, and armament all complemented each other and performed to the optimum.

The war in the Pacific ended in August 1945, and with it the need for a larger number of warships, however recently constructed. The *Fletcher*s fell into this category on both counts, and so they, along with all preceding classes, became surplus and began to be laid up. By the end of 1946, the entire class, with the exception of a handful kept in commission for training duties, had been cocooned and laid up in reserve. In terms of naval architecture, they were very modern ships, but in another way were obsolete in that they lacked the necessary internal volume to accommodate all the latest equipment that the war had forced into development. Although they were big enough for ASW warfare, they were not big enough to be suitable as modern fleet destroyers and were not fitted out with the equipment that the postwar ASW scene demanded. They were, therefore, kept in reserve as part of a mobilization force that could be called upon in any future emergency.

Onset of the Cold War

Of the military technical revolution that World War II spawned, one of the far-reaching aspects was the invention and development, almost to the point of being put in operation, of the next generation of submarines, illustrated by the German Type 21. Here for the first time was a true submersible fighting vessel, one that could sustain actions completely under water and at very high speed. So revolutionary was this development that at one stroke it made almost 100 percent of the Allied ASW vessels out-of-date.

The Soviets had captured these German submarines at war's end, and it was the great fear of the Allies in the late forties that within a few years they would be faced with several hundred Soviet submarines roaming the Atlantic with the potential to cut the transatlantic lifeline with far less effort than the World War II German fleet had to exert.

In the U. S. Navy, the only ships really suitable for conversion into modern ASW ships would be the *Sumner*s, *Gearing*s, and *Fletcher*s. The *Sumner*s and *Gearing*s were needed for fleet work, though, and there were not enough of them anyway. This left the *Fletcher*s—of modern construction—with a high enough speed and with enough internal volume to allow a proper ASW conversion.

The expected Soviet threat did not emerge like the expected race horse out of the starting gate, but more like the slightly awkward tortoise. But before the tortoise had been identified as such, a whole series of U. S. programs were proposed in 1948 in answer to the threat, one of which was the conversion of every *Fletcher* into an ASW destroyer (DDE). And although by 1950 the navy had revised its evaluation of a future Soviet threat drastically downwards, a few *Fletcher*s were put into dockyard hands for a full ASW conversion, included in which was the requirement that they carry the MK 108 antisubmarine (rocket) launcher in place of the No. 2 5-inch mount. However, the MK 108 suffered from developmental problems and slow production, and the appearance of the *Fletchers* as DDEs saw them fitted with the trainable MK 15 hedgehog instead.

The Bofors guns were removed, and in their place two twin 3-inch automatic mountings were provided for AA fire. The deckhouses on the main deck were enlarged, one of the most important internal additons being the inclusion of ASW homing torpedoes. These were fired out of portals from tubes arranged in the midships deckhouse; the circular hatches can be seen on the drawings of the *Renshaw*, with the internal layout shown on the main-deck plan view.

The Korean "police" action that erupted in 1950 necessitated the activation of the *Fletchers*, and once more they were back in action. Those of the class not earmarked for DDE conversion were given an austere refit, including slightly updated electronics and the replacement of the forward pair of twin Bofors, with two MK 10 fixed hedgehogs.

The end of the Korean War in 1953 did not see the class going back into reserve as had the end of World War II. The bulk of the class stayed active, with further DDE conversions undertaken and many others staying in service as all-gun ships, but with 3-inch twin mountings instead of Bofors, and up-to-date sensors. The remainder, those that kept five 5-inch guns and two Bofors mountings, rotated through periods of reserve and service until well into the 1960s.

Three of the class were selected for a Fleet Rehabilitation Modernization (FRAM). This involved a complete reconstruction of the superstructure abaft the second stack, with a comprehensive hangar and facility added, to accommodate two DASH helicopters.

The 1960s saw *Fletchers* still on active service, but a growing number were either sold to other nations or stricken from the navy lists and subsequently scrapped. In the late sixties, there was a wholesale disposal of the class, with only a few surviving into the seventies, in the active Naval Reserve Force. By the end of the decade, none were left on the U.S. Naval Vessel Register lists. They had all been broken up or sold to foreign navies, with the exception of three preserved as memorials—the *Kidd*, *Sullivans*, and *Cassin Young*.

Particulars (1942)

LOA	376'6"
LWL	369'0"
Beam	39'8"
SHP	60,000
Speed (at 2,800 tons displacement)	35 knots
Endurance (estimated)	4,800 NM/at 15 knots
Displacement (design)	2,700 tons
Complement	273 officers and men
Armament	five 5-inch 38-caliber DP guns ten 21-inch torpedo tubes AA weapons (see text)

Photographs

Still on the stocks, but approaching the final fitting out stage, the *Saufley* on 4 July 1942 at Federal Shipbuilding & Dry Dock Co., at Kearny, New Jersey.

Even if a ship was not the actual target of a kamikaze, the suicide plane could still be dangerous. In these two views, the *Halsey Powell*, while steaming close alongside the carrier *Hancock*, is scraped on the stern by a kamikaze on its way to explode in the carrier's side. The second view shows the *Halsey Powell* retiring from the scene, damaged and down by the stern, but still able to steam and fight.

While giving fire support at Iwo Jima, the *Hall* struck a mine forward, but in spite of extensive damage, the ship survived.

Destroyers always had to look out for themselves when driving in traffic. In this view, taken on 16 April 1945, the carrier *Intrepid* was hit by a kamikaze. The carrier began to execute a radial high-speed turn, and the escorting destroyer is about to turn across her bow, while also making a high-speed turn. Both vessels are making around 30 knots.

In spite of ships operating well inside enemy waters, the mail was always delivered. This picture shows the *Cushing* coming alongside the cruiser *Baltimore* to arrange a pickup. Photo taken in February 1945 during the second carrier raid on Tokyo.

When steaming alongside, it was very important to maintain as much as possible an unvarying distance from the larger vessel, something that a transferring person appreciated.

In this picture, mail is in the actual process of being transferred. The ship is the *Harrison*.

While operating off Okinawa, the *Newcomb* and *Sigsbee* took kamikaze hits, but both survived.

The kamikazes dealt particularly savage blows, especially to the smaller ships. Here, the *Hazelwood* has been "crashed" right by the bridge. Her captain and 45 others were killed, but she was able to steam after emergency repairs. The attending destroyer is the *Colahan*.

The *Stephen Potter* about to begin refueling from a tanker.

The torpedo director in use. Every ship in the war period had two of these, one in each bridge wing.

A close-up angle of the early postwar arrangement for DF antennas carried on the aft stack; later on a more substantial construction using a bipod mast was fitted in ships that underwent a more involved refit. The ship shown here is the *Cassin Young*.

The Okinawan campaign produced heavy human casualties, and in this May 1945 view, the destroyer *Sullivans* is seen transferring wounded to the hospital ship *Repose*.

The throttle board in the *Heywood L. Edwards*.

WW II destroyers had crowded interiors, and the pilothouse, seen here, was no exception. Photo taken on board the *Heywood L. Edwards*.

A most interesting view of *Fletcher*s being laid up in January 1946 at Mare Island. The middle and outboard vessels show the webbing over the equipment prior to being covered.

Soon after the end of the war in August 1945, the entire class was laid up in reserve, and it was only in 1949 that the first few were taken in hand for ASW conversion. In this picture, the *Nicholas* is shown being transferred to the refit yard to undergo such a conversion.

A closeup of the ECM mainmast fit of the *Morrison*, taken upon completion of a refit at Hunters Point in February 1945.

In the mid-1943 refit of the *Fullam*, twin Bofors were added in front of the bridge along with the associated Mk 51 directors, seen here positioned on the roof of the pilothouse.

(*Right*) A beautiful shot looking down into the bridge area of the *Young*, taken during her July 1945 refit. This picture shows how crowded these ships were by war's end.

As part of the Navy's expansion program, the yards of the Seattle Tacoma Shipbuilding Corp. were expanded considerably, with many orders going to them for *Fletcher*s. Seen here is the *Franks* during final fitting out in July 1945. Note the arrangements forward of the bridge for three single 20-mm mountings.

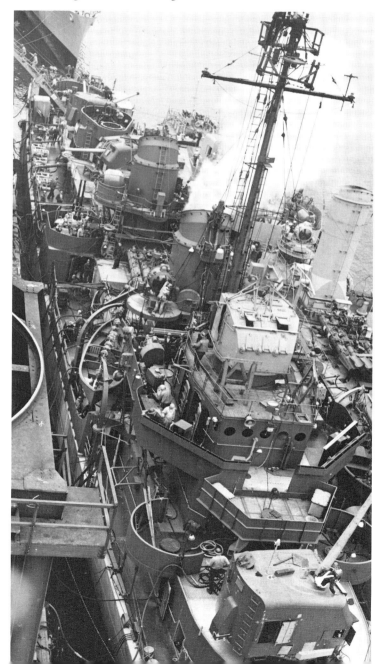

Three views of the *Radford* upon completion of a January 1944 refit, greatly changed from her mid-1942 as-built appearance.

When the Navy moved into the nuclear age, washing-down equipment was installed as a method of removing radioactive dust that may have been deposited on the ship's structure during an engagement. The *Walker* is seen here during washing-down trials in 1955.

Looking into the rear of the bridge of the *Yarnall* in June 1945 during a refit.

The aft part of the *Charles Ausburne* upon completion of her September 1944 refit. In this period the first mainmast ESM/ECM installations were made. Later installations were more extensive, as shown by the other photographs.

Two views of the *Heermann* in January 1945. Additions include an ECM/ESM mainmast, and a repositioning of the torpedo director in the bridge wings.

Many vessels languished in storage areas long after being stricken. In this view, the *Wiley* is shown being towed out of San Diego in April 1970 to the breakers' yard, in spite of being officially struck from the lists in 1968.

Two angles of the *Gatling* laid up at Philadelphia Navy Yard in 1975. Decommissioned in 1960, she remained in reserve until stricken in 1974.

In 1943, three *Fletcher*s received an aircraft catapult as shown by the photo of the *Stevens*. This equipment was removed after only a few months, and although the No. 3 5-inch gun was then installed, the ships had to wait until later to receive the aft superstructure and the 40-mm Bofors. As an interim measure, the three ships carried two single 20-mm mountings between Nos. 3 and 4 5-inch mounting, as illustrated by this view of the *Pringle* in early 1944.

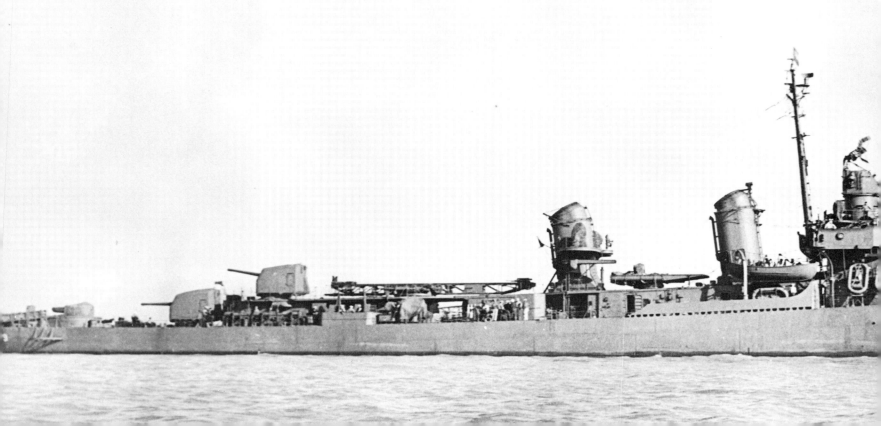

A quarter aerial view of the *Burns* at sea after her 1944 refit. She has the full AA armament of ten Bofors and seven 20 mm.

1944 saw a large-scale application of disruptive camouflage schemes to ships of the Pacific. The *Colhoun* illustrates just how dramatic these paint schemes looked; the photo was taken in July 1944 upon completion.

The *Isherwood* shows the final wartime configuration of the *Fletchers*, with three twin Bofors, two quadruple Bofors, one set of torpedo tubes, six twin 20 mm, and an extensive ESM/ECM installation on the main and maintopmast.

*Fletcher*s in reserve were periodically taken out for overhaul. About to undergo such is the *O'Bannon*, seen here at Long Beach Navy Yard in January 1949.

A few of the class were used for reserve training, and these tended to receive the minimum of refitting and updating. The *David W. Taylor* is seen here at San Francisco in 1957 with few changes from her wartime appearance.

The *John D. Henley* under construction on 3 January 1943 at Gulf Shipbuilding Corp., Chickasaw, Alabama.

Seen here is the *Luce* on the 21st of June 1943, her commissioning day.
Photo taken at N.Y. Navy Yard.

Looking along the length of the *William D. Porter* during turning trails out of Charleston, S.C., in September 1943.

The *Jenkins* being delivered from the builders on 30 July 1942 without radar and Bofors mountings.

The *Jenkins* in January 1944 upon completion of her refit. The white circles indicate the changes made at this time.

There was the occasional need for the Bureau of Ships to ascertain displacements, which necessitated an inclining test. The *Philip* is shown here undergoing such a test prior to delivery. Picture taken on 15 November 1942.

Although the *Pringle* was fitted with an aircraft catapult, she commissioned without it, and it was not installed until a little later. She was the only known *Fletcher* to be fitted with a SA air-search radar, the antenna for which is carried at the masthead.

The *Jenkins* after her N.Y. Navy Yard fitting out; photo taken on 17 August 1942.

A late square-bridge *Fletcher* (name unknown) after launch. This ship is already fitted for five 40-mm Bofors, and so this view was probably taken in late 1943.

The *Saufley* in late 1942 upon completion of her N.Y. Navy Yard fitting out, which included two twin Bofors and radar.

One of the interim AA arrangements of three twin Bofors and ten 20-mm mounts is shown here in this view of the *McCord* taken upon completion on 29 August 1943.

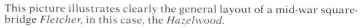

This picture illustrates clearly the general layout of a mid-war square-bridge *Fletcher*, in this case, the *Hazelwood*.

When the single 20-mm mountings were replaced by twins, one single position on the fantail was deleted. This meant that the depth-charge tracks could be lengthened and the 20-mm bulwark shape changed, seen here in this photo of the *Capps* in September 1945.

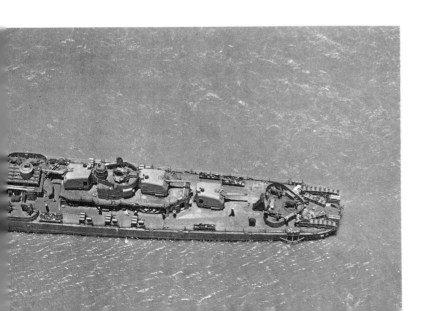

A builder's view of the *Yarnall* taken on 17 January 1944. She is fitted for five twin Bofors mountings, but only four have been installed; the after centerline mounting has not yet been fitted.

In the months following the end of the Pacific war, the ships gradually changed from wartime to peacetime colors. Here, the *Stanly* repaints from the overall dark navy blue to peacetime light grey.

Fletchers that were delivered in the last months of 1942 and early months of 1943 usually had two twin Bofors and four single 20-mm mounts fitted. There was also a change from the measure 12 modified camouflage of dappled or mottled pattern to two-tone measure 22 as shown by the Beale on her way from the builders to N.Y. Navy Yard.

(Below) Of all the Fletchers active into the sixties, only three were taken in hand for a FRAM refit; one of these was the Jenkins, seen here off Hawaii in May 1962.

(Below) In the late 1950s the *Hazelwood* was chosen to be the test ship for DASH operations, and to this end, the aft superstructure was completely remodeled to incorporate a hangar and associated platform. She served in this mode from 1958 to 1965.

(Above) Comparing this view of *Renshaw* to the drawings of her, one can see that the Mk 15 hedgehog has been replaced by a Mk 108 launcher. Another change is the bipod mainmast just in front of the second funnel.

Many of the class received postwar refits that maintained an emphasis on the gunnery aspect of war, as illustrated by this picture of the *Sullivans* taken in the early 1960s. The bridge walkway has been covered over, twin 3-inch added, the Bofors removed along with one set of torpedo tubes. Only one 5-inch mounting has been removed, and she has an up-to-date radar fit in the form of the large SPS-6C radar on the foremast, the SPS-10 above it, and a comprehensive outfit of ECM/ESM and communications gear.

In spite of being completely obsolete, many *Fletcher*s, including the *Sullivans*, retained the WW II Mk 10 hedgehog. The hedgehog was first in service in the spring of 1941 on the *Westcott*, a British destroyer, and by the fifties was completely out-of-date.

The *Conway* underway in Hampton Roads in June 1965, showing her as an ASW vessel. This view shows clearly the deck arrangements and rigging details.

The *Isherwood* at speed out of San Francisco—date unknown—but probably taken in the early 1950s. She is still a five-gun vessel and retains her midship quad, and aft twin Bofors, along with the mid-1945 ECM/ESM mainmast arrangement. She retains the wartime SC-4 radar, but has been fitted with the SU radar at the foremast top, so that apart from the SU and removal of the forward Bofors and the two hedgehogs in their location, she is a destroyer still with only WW II capabilities.

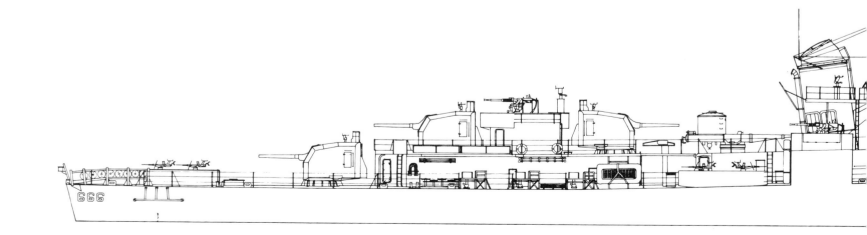

Drawings

USS *Black*

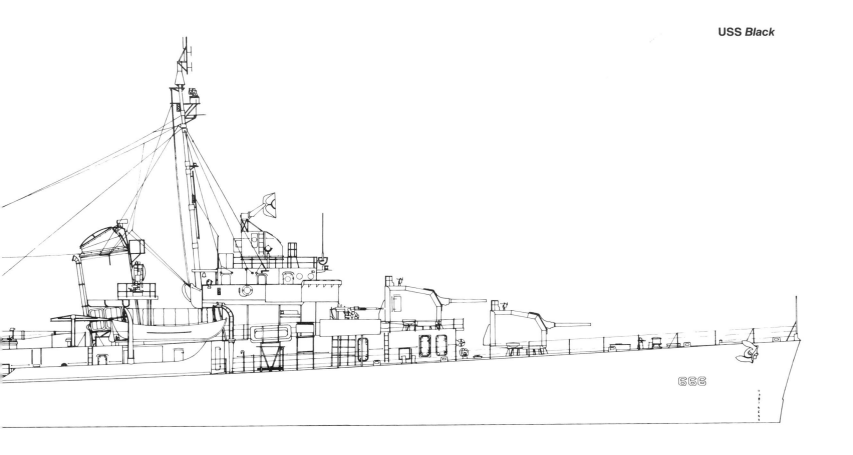

666

A. GENERAL ARRANGEMENT PLANS

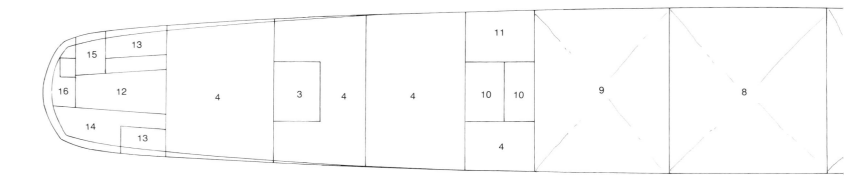

General key

vertical ladder	=	
20-mm gun position	=	+
door	=	
indicates line of platform over	=	- - - - -

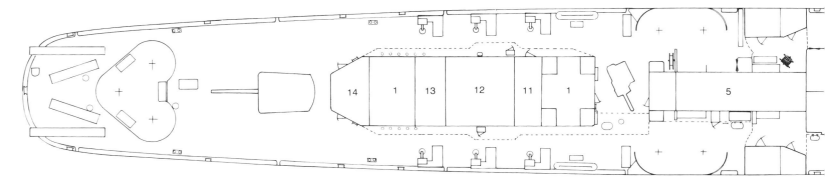

USS *Black*—1st Platform Deck

1. Cable locker
2. CPO's mess
3. 5″ handling room
4. Cabins
5. CIC & plotting room
6. Office
7. Office
8. Boiler room
9. Engine room
10. Workshop
11. Workshop
12. Steering-geer room
13. Locker
14. Carpenter shop
15. 20-mm clipping room
16. Smoke generating compartment

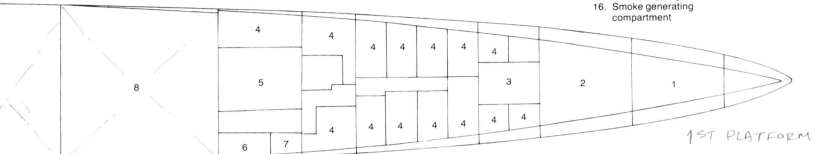

1ST PLATFORM

USS *Black*—Main Deck

1. 5″ handling room
2. Wardroom & messroom
3. Stateroom
4. CIC
5. Uptake space
6. Galley
7. Laundry
8. Battery charging room
9. Emergency radio room
10. Supply office
11. Passage
12. Crew's washroom
13. Crew's W.C.
14. Locker space

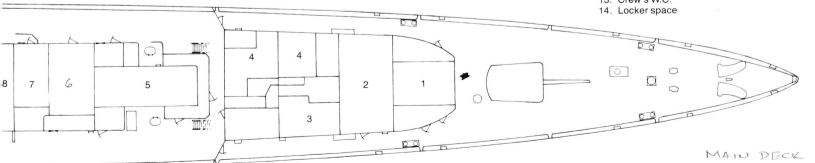

MAIN DECK

Two refit views of the *Owen* during here August 1945 refit. Seen here are the two quadruple Bofors mountings positioned amidships as part of the anti-kamikaze program. Other changes are: twin for single 20-mm mountings; radar intercept aerials fitted to the aft funnel, and to the face of the pilothouse; a mainmast dedicated to ECM/ESM aerials, and extra short-wave communication antennas on the foremast.

USS *Black*—2nd Platform Deck & Hold

2nd Platform Deck
Hold

Key to navigating bridge
1. Pilothouse
2. Fire-control station
3. Captain's sea cabin

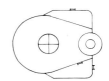

Key to superstructure deck
1. 40-mm ready-service room
2. Coding room
3. Radio central
4. Chart stowage
5. 40-mm ready-service room
6. Gun crew shelter
7. Fan room

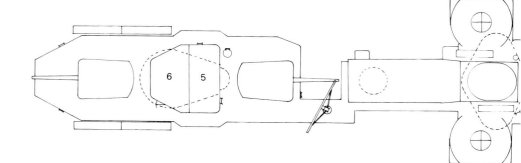

Key to 2nd Platform Deck
1. Stores
2. Crew's quarters
3. Fuel-oil service tank
4. Battle-dressing station
5. Crew's mess
6. Diesel generating room
7. Stores
8. Boiler room
9. Engine room
10. Fuel-oil service tank
11. Diesel oil
12. Fuel oil
13. 5″ handling room
14. 40-mm magazine
15. 5″ powder magazine
16. Chemical-warfare material

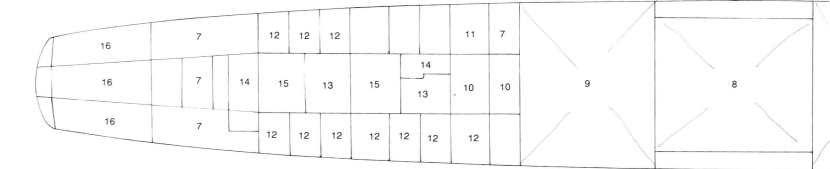

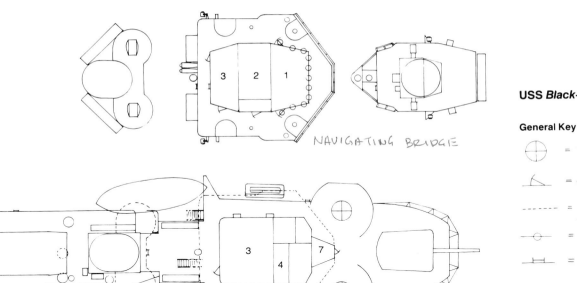

NAVIGATING BRIDGE

SUPER STRUCTURE DECK

USS *Black*—Superstructure Deck

General Key

⊕ = twin Bofors

◿ = door

------ = indicates line of platform over or mounting

⊖ = scuttle

⊢⊣ = vertical ladder

HOLD

2ND PLATFORM

Key to Hold

1. Peak tank	10. Cofferdam
2. Paint store	11. Reserve feedwater
3. Stores	12. Fresh water
4. Sonar compartment	13. Boiler room
5. Small-arms magazine	14. Engine room
6. 40-mm magazine	15. Sump tank
7. Void	16. Diesel oil
8. Fuel oil	17. Stores
9. Oil service tank	18. Fuel oil separating tank

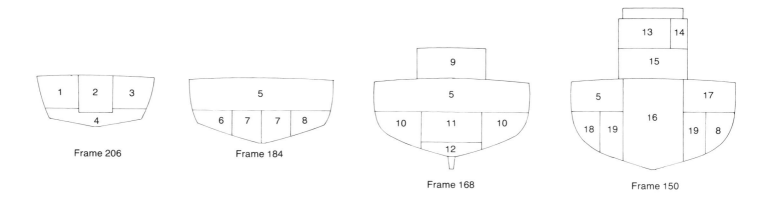

Frame 206

Frame 184

Frame 168

Frame 150

On board the *La Vallette* in October 1942 upon completion of the second N.Y. Navy Yard refit, during which she received the Mk 51 director for her fantail-fitted Bofors.

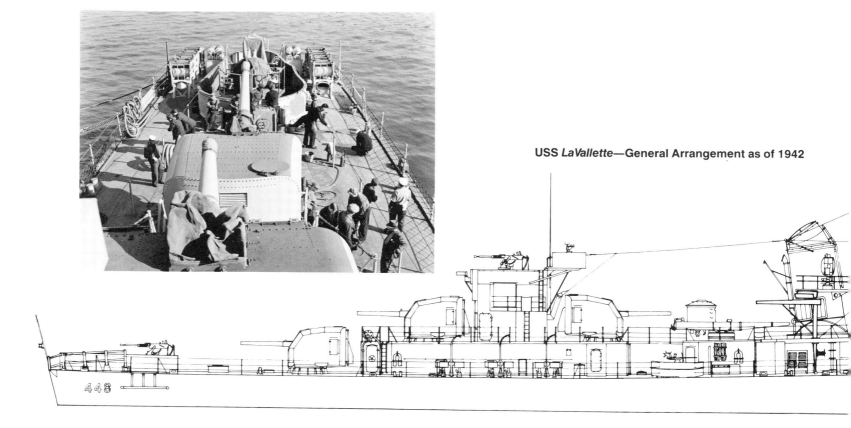

USS *LaVallette*—General Arrangement as of 1942

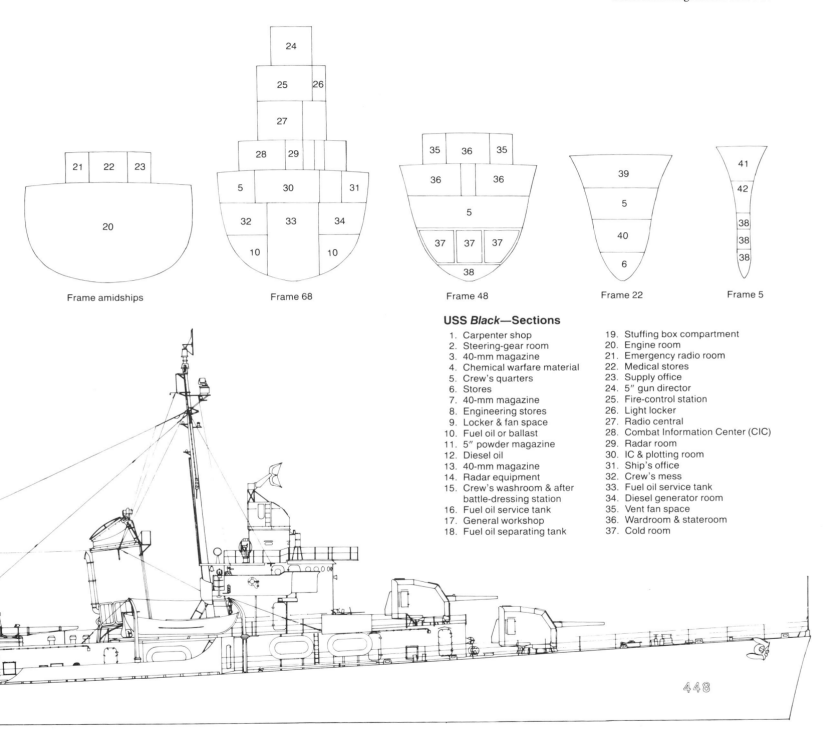

Frame amidships

Frame 68

Frame 48

Frame 22

Frame 5

USS *Black*—Sections

1. Carpenter shop
2. Steering-gear room
3. 40-mm magazine
4. Chemical warfare material
5. Crew's quarters
6. Stores
7. 40-mm magazine
8. Engineering stores
9. Locker & fan space
10. Fuel oil or ballast
11. 5″ powder magazine
12. Diesel oil
13. 40-mm magazine
14. Radar equipment
15. Crew's washroom & after battle-dressing station
16. Fuel oil service tank
17. General workshop
18. Fuel oil separating tank
19. Stuffing box compartment
20. Engine room
21. Emergency radio room
22. Medical stores
23. Supply office
24. 5″ gun director
25. Fire-control station
26. Light locker
27. Radio central
28. Combat Information Center (CIC)
29. Radar room
30. IC & plotting room
31. Ship's office
32. Crew's mess
33. Fuel oil service tank
34. Diesel generator room
35. Vent fan space
36. Wardroom & stateroom
37. Cold room

Twin 40-mm
Gun Platform

Aft Steering
Position

Searchlight
Platform

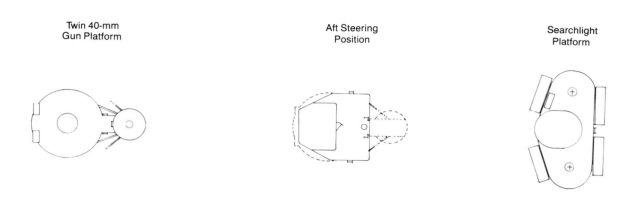

Superstructure Deck

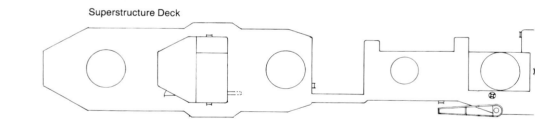

Main Deck

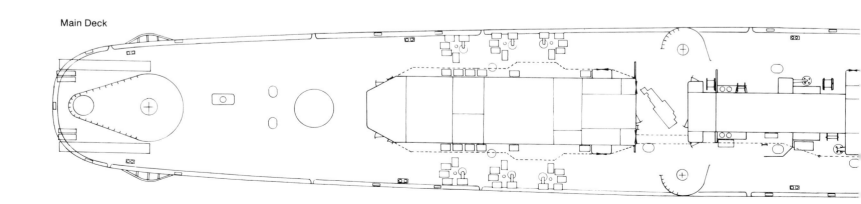

Navigating
Bridge

Pilothouse
Roof

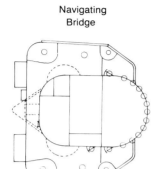

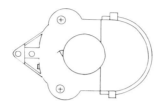

USS *LaVallette*

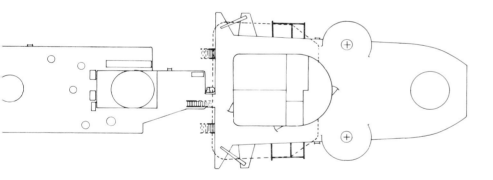

USS *LaVallette*

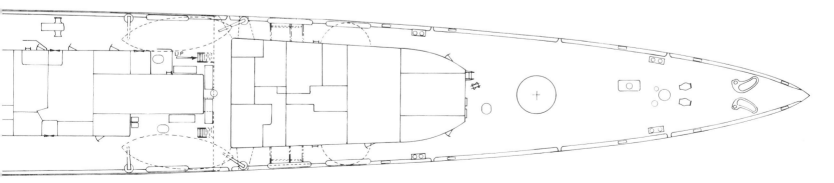

A close-up of the early style of the high aft superstructure. The canvas-covered object is the 1.1″ quad mounting fitted to only three ships of the class—the *Fletcher, Nicholas,* and *O'Bannon.*

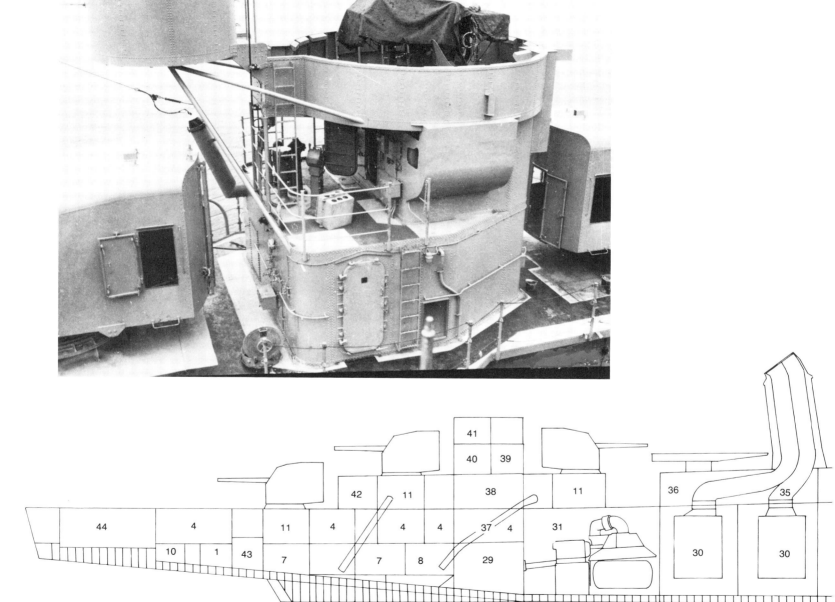

Rear view of the aft stack of the *Jenkins* while undergoing the post-builder's refit at N.Y. Navy Yard in August 1942 before going operational.

USS *LaVallette*—Inboard Profile

1.	Stores	23.	Pilothouse
2.	Peak tank	24.	Sonar room
3.	Underwater sound room	25.	Captain's sea cabin
4.	Crew's quarters	26.	Fire-control station
5.	Crew's W.C.s	27.	5″ director
6.	CPO's mess	28.	Fuel oil
7.	5″ powder magazine	29.	Fuel oil
8.	5″ shell magazine	30.	Boiler
9.	40-mm magazine	31.	Engine room
10.	Small-arms magazine	32.	Galley
11.	5″ handling room	33.	Laundry
12.	CPO's W.C.s	34.	Emergency radio room
13.	Officers' quarters	35.	Uptakes
14.	Cold room	36.	Torpedo workshop
15.	Fuel oil	37.	Shell & powder hoist
16.	Crew's mess	38.	Crew's washroom
17.	Officers' quarters	39.	40-mm ready-service room
18.	Captain's stateroom	40.	Fan room
18A.	Wardroom	41.	Emergency steering position
19.	Radar room	42.	Fan space
20.	Radio central	43.	40-mm magazine
21.	Coding room	44.	Steering-gear room
22.	Gun crew shelter		

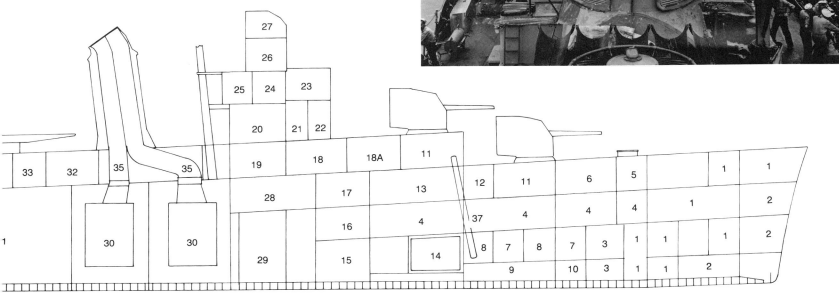

Before and after; the first picture shows *La Vallette* on 11 August 1942 en route to N.Y. Navy Yard from the builders. She lacks radar and the 40-mm Bofors in the aft structure. In the second view, she appears on 5 September 1942 after refit, during which two 20-mm have been removed from the waist, two twin Bofors added aft, and air and surface and gunnery radar fitted. To accommodate the Bofors on the fantail, the depth-charge tracks have been moved farther outboard.

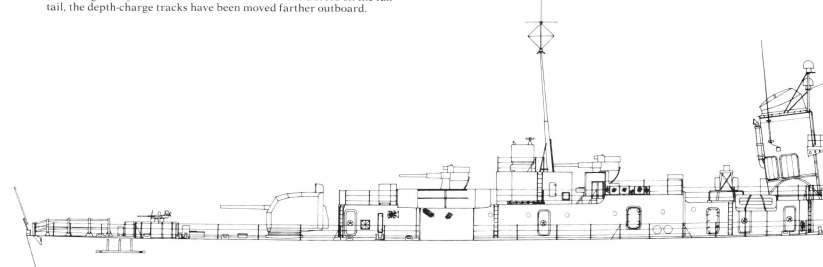

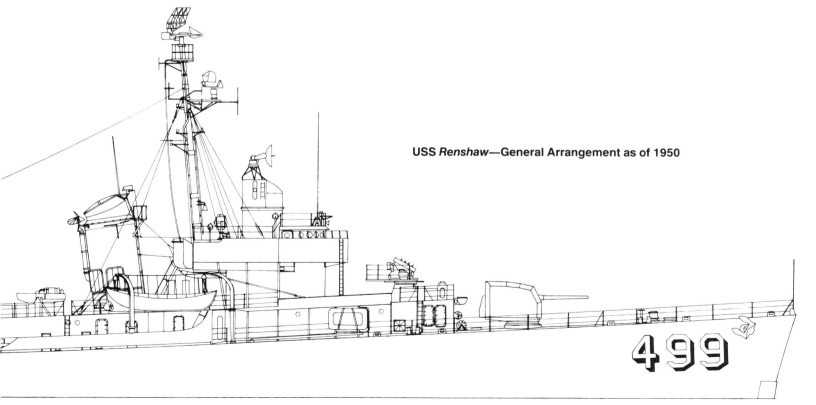

USS *Renshaw*—General Arrangement as of 1950

USS *Renshaw*
Superstructure Deck

Twin 3" Mounts P & S

Main Deck

TORPEDO ROOM

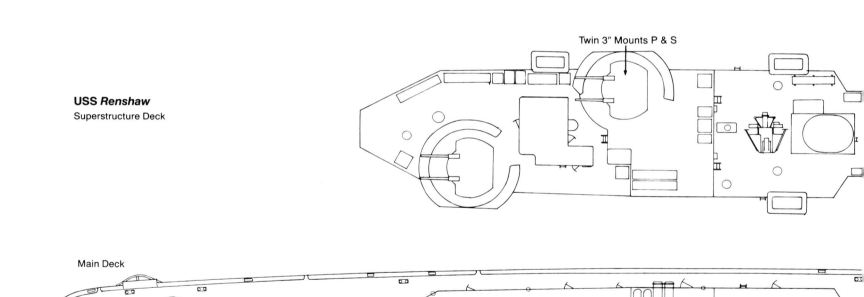

Pilothouse

USS *Renshaw*

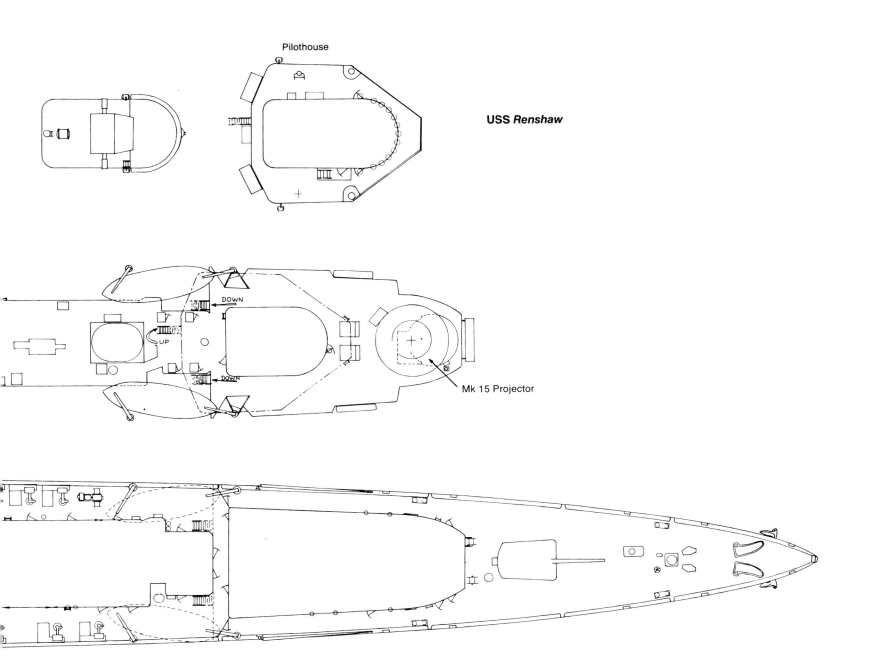

DOWN

UP

DOWN

Mk 15 Projector

When the midship Bofors were fitted to the class, the torpedo crane that was originally positioned in this location had to be moved forward, and a second crane of lighter design, one that was telescopic, was added between the midship and aft deckhouses, seen here on the *Fullam* during her July 1943 refit.

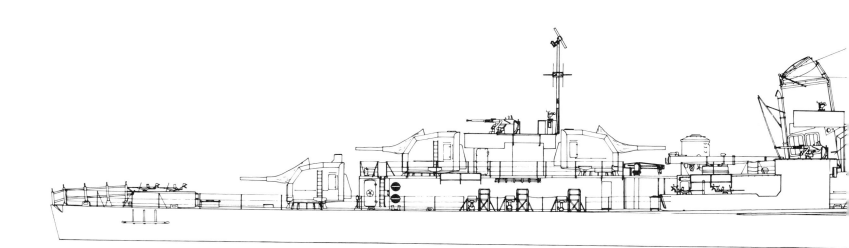

Complementing the drawings are two aerials of the *Fullam* during her late 1944 refit. The major change from her 1943 refit (see other photos) is the addition of a mainmast to carry ECM/ESM antennas.

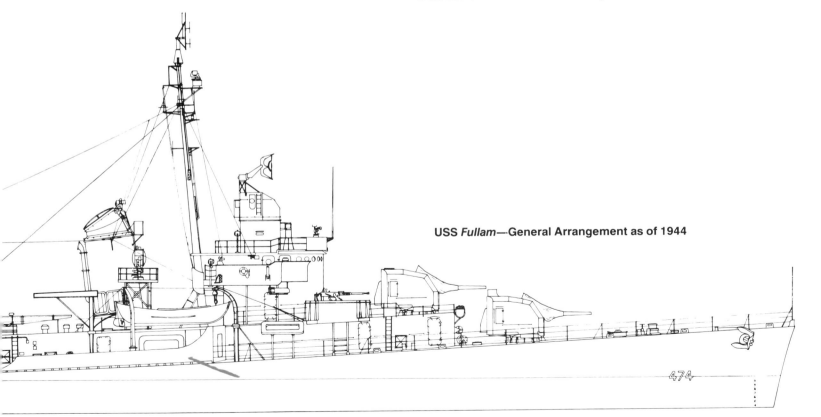

USS *Fullam*—General Arrangement as of 1944

474

USS _Fullam_

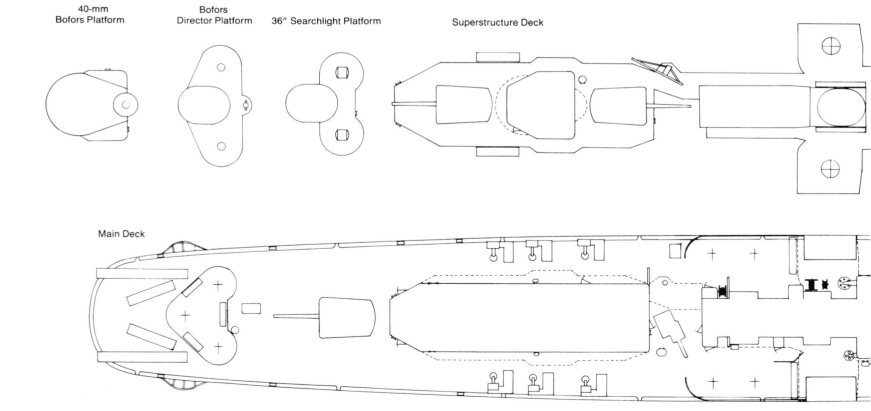

40-mm
Bofors Platform

Bofors
Director Platform

36″ Searchlight Platform

Superstructure Deck

Main Deck

Navigating Bridge

Roof of Pilothouse

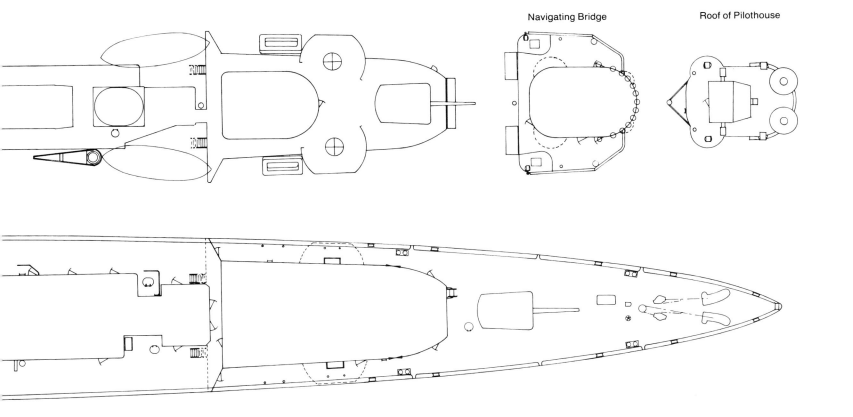

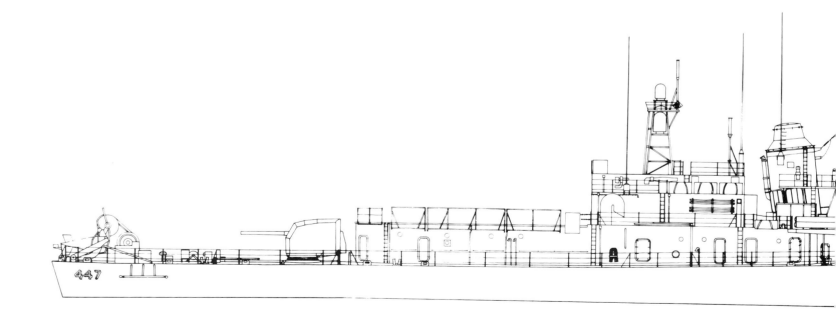

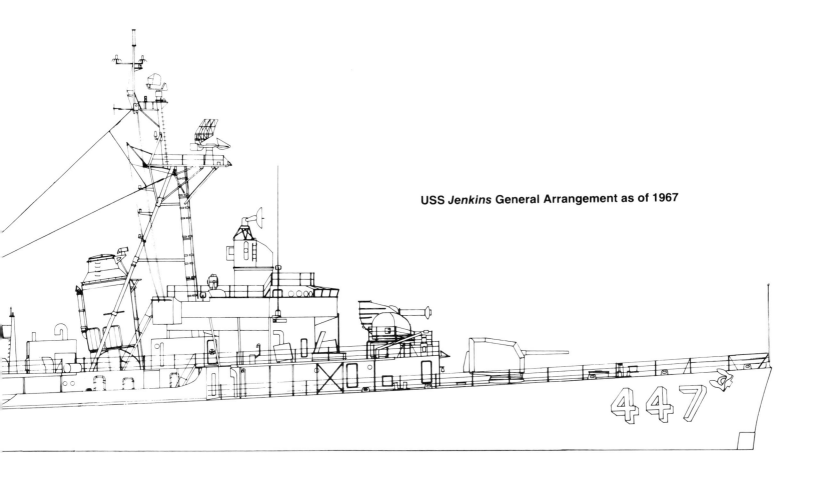

USS *Jenkins* General Arrangement as of 1967

USS *Jenkins*

Key to Superstructure Deck
1. Coding room
2. Passage
3. Radio central
4. Cabin
5. Radio transmitter room
6. Helicopter hangar
7. Torpedo stowage house

Key to Main Deck
1. Rocket ready service room
2. Wardroom & messroom
3. Pantry
4. Captain's stateroom
5. Radar room
6. Radar room
7. Radar IFF room
8. Small arms locker
9. Vegetable locker
10. Uptake space
11. Deck gear locker
12. Barber shop
13. Galley
14. Laundry
15. Issue room
16. Battery charging room
17. Fan room
18. Passage
19. Sick bay
20. Auxiliary radio room
21. Office
22. Electronic shop
23. ECM room
24. Torpedo room
25. Staterooms
26. Wardrooms & staterooms
27. Crews living space
28. Crews WC's & showers
29. Crews wardroom & battle dressing station

Roof of Hangar

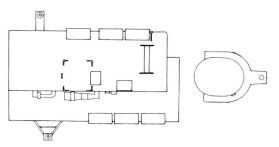

Superstructure Deck

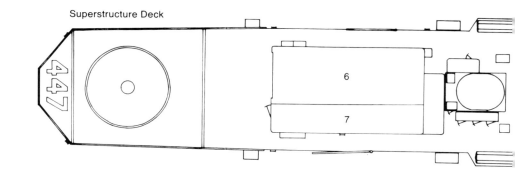

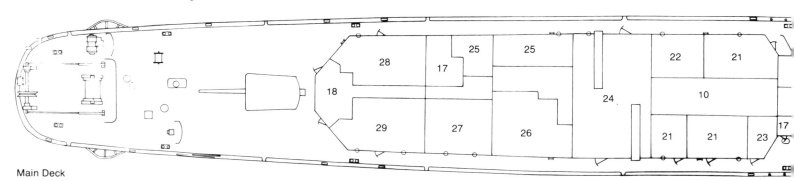

Main Deck

USS *Jenkins*

Key to Pilothouse
1. Pilothouse
2. Captain's sea cabin
3. CIC

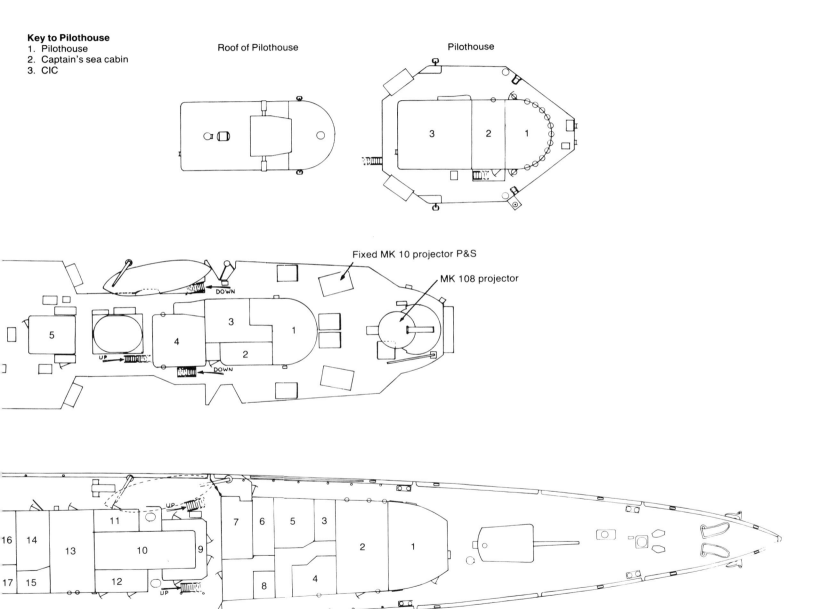

Roof of Pilothouse

Pilothouse

Fixed MK 10 projector P&S

MK 108 projector

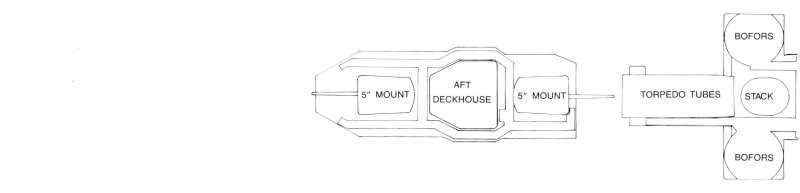

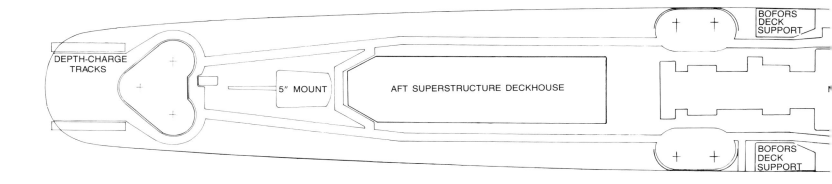

Sheer Plan

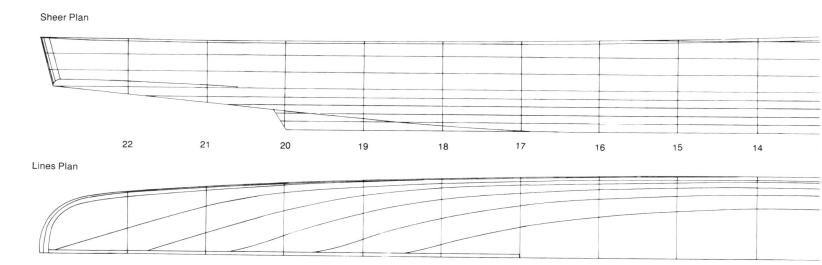

Lines Plan

General Arrangement of Main &
Superstructure Decks
Showing Layout of Non-Slip Walkways
Laid onto the Decks

Although this arrangement was
generally followed, there were many
exceptions, as shown in the photos of
deck views.

KWAYS PORT & STARBOARD

EDO TUBES   STACK

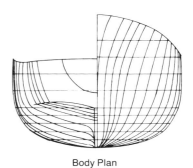

Body Plan

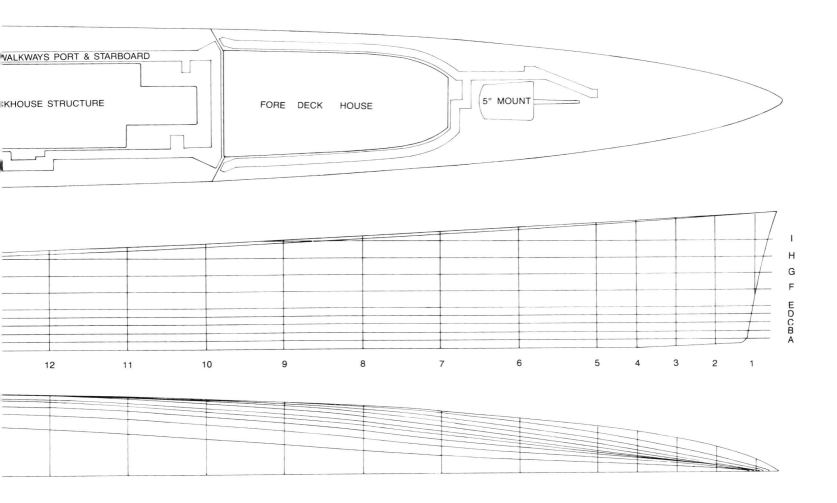

WALKWAYS PORT & STARBOARD

KHOUSE STRUCTURE   FORE   DECK   HOUSE   5" MOUNT

I
H
G
F
E
D
C
B
A

12   11   10   9   8   7   6   5   4   3   2   1

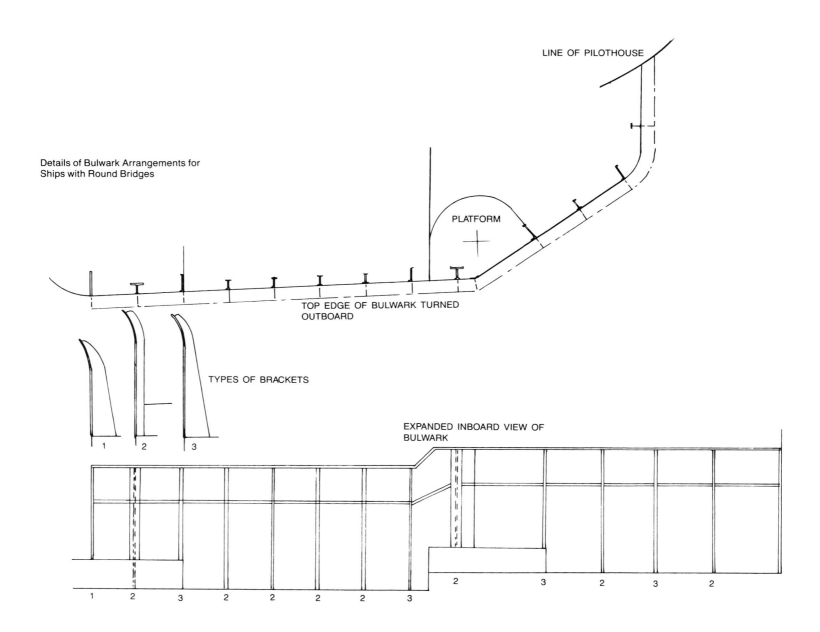

LINE OF PILOTHOUSE

Details of Bulwark Arrangements for
Ships with Round Bridges

PLATFORM

TOP EDGE OF BULWARK TURNED
OUTBOARD

TYPES OF BRACKETS

1   2   3

EXPANDED INBOARD VIEW OF
BULWARK

1   2   3   2   2   2   2   3

2   3   2   3   2

Details of Bulwark Arrangements for
Ships with Square Bridges

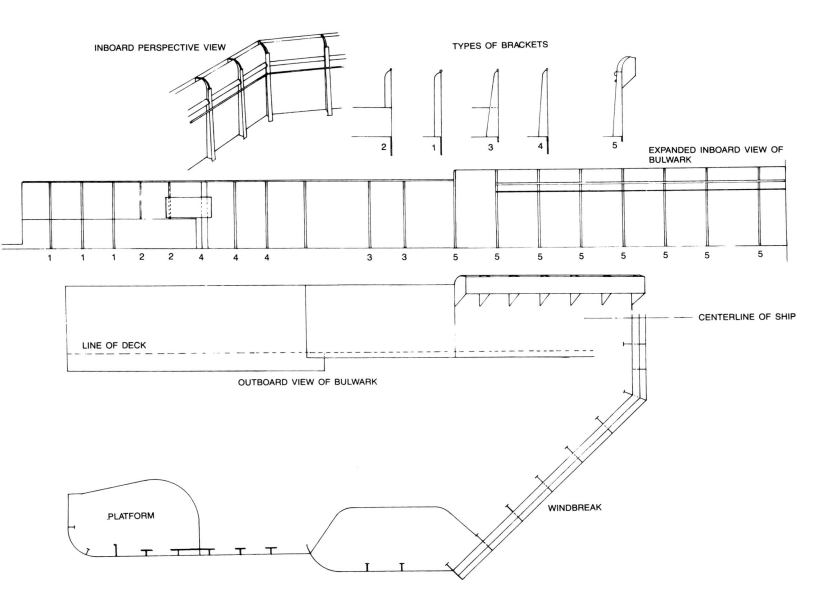

INBOARD PERSPECTIVE VIEW

TYPES OF BRACKETS

2   1   3   4   5

EXPANDED INBOARD VIEW OF
BULWARK

1   1   1   2   2   4   4   4   3   3   5   5   5   5   5   5   5   5

CENTERLINE OF SHIP

LINE OF DECK

OUTBOARD VIEW OF BULWARK

WINDBREAK

PLATFORM

B. GENERAL FITTINGS & EQUIPMENT

Two of these were normally carried on the roof of the bridge toward the aft end, but as ships gained weight and were refitted, they were generally removed.

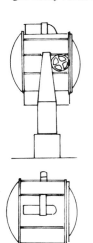

24″ Searchlight

To obtain proficiency in the loading and operation of the 5″ guns, every ship was equipped with a 5″ practice loader. Basically, it was an operating breach mechanism mounted at the same height as the real gun. During the war, this equipment was placed between the midship and aft deckhouses, but in postwar conversions (that demanded enlarged and additional deck structures), the loader was moved, usually to the top of the midship deckhouse between the stacks.

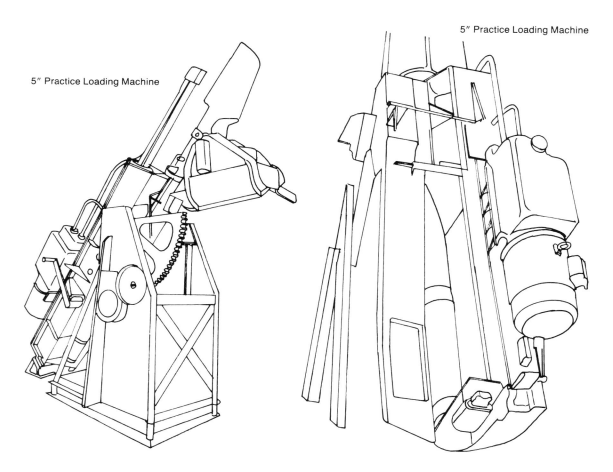

5″ Practice Loading Machine

5″ Practice Loading Machine

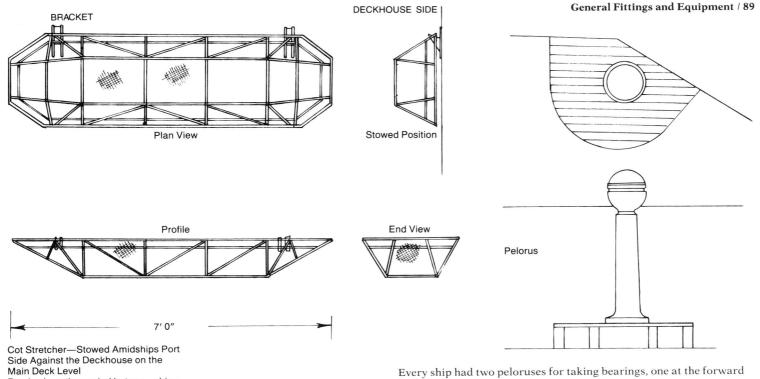

BRACKET

Plan View

DECKHOUSE SIDE

Stowed Position

Profile

End View

Pelorus

7' 0"

Cot Stretcher—Stowed Amidships Port
Side Against the Deckhouse on the
Main Deck Level
Precise Location varied between ships

Every ship had two peloruses for taking bearings, one at the forward
end of each bridge wing.

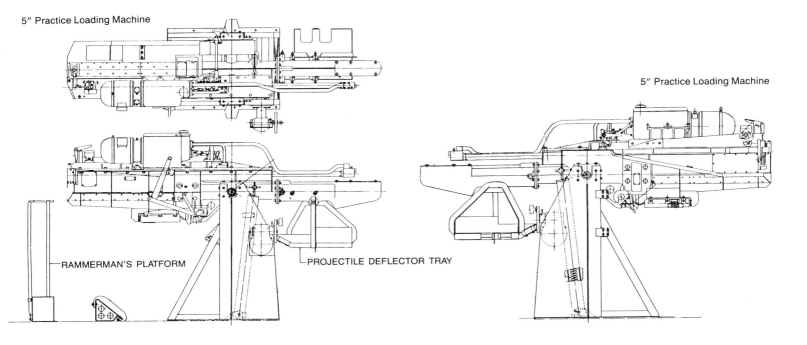

5" Practice Loading Machine

5" Practice Loading Machine

RAMMERMAN'S PLATFORM

PROJECTILE DEFLECTOR TRAY

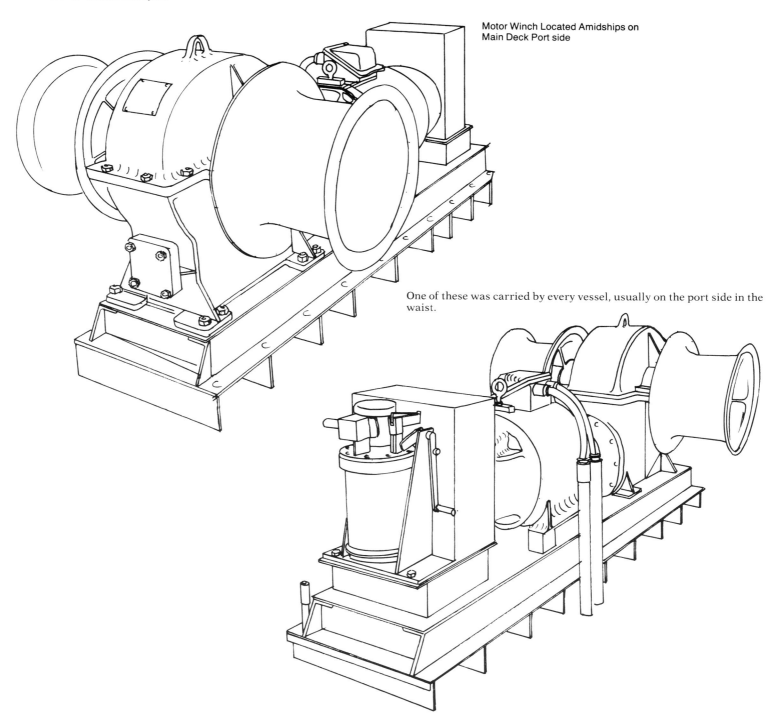

Motor Winch Located Amidships on
Main Deck Port side

One of these was carried by every vessel, usually on the port side in the waist.

In early ships, two of these were fitted at the rear ends of the bridge wings, but as later ships entered service and earlier ones were refitted, the number and position varied from ship to ship.

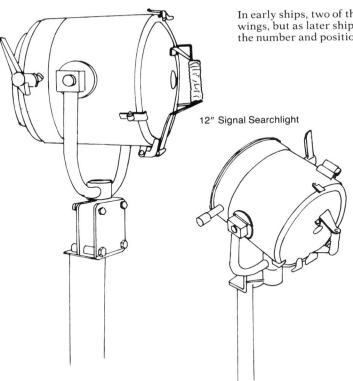

12″ Signal Searchlight

Every ship was fitted with a pair of smoke generators at the stern between the depth-charge racks. Beginning in early 1945, these were replaced by a below-deck system where the smoke was fed through a conduit to a circular dispenser some six feet above the deck.

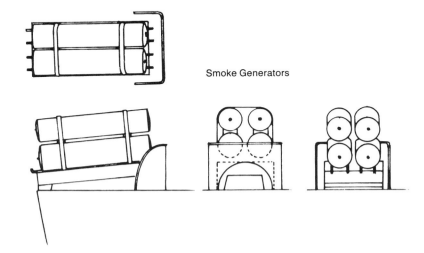

Smoke Generators

Ready Use Locker for 20-mm Mounting

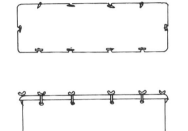

Ready Use Locker for Hedgehog Mounting

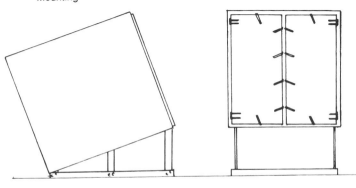

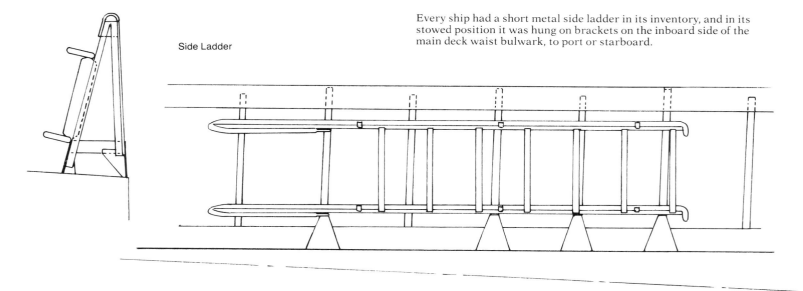

Side Ladder

Every ship had a short metal side ladder in its inventory, and in its stowed position it was hung on brackets on the inboard side of the main deck waist bulwark, to port or starboard.

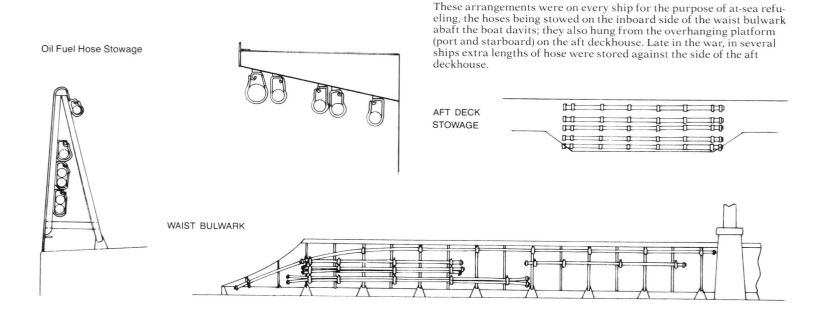

Oil Fuel Hose Stowage

These arrangements were on every ship for the purpose of at-sea refueling, the hoses being stowed on the inboard side of the waist bulwark abaft the boat davits; they also hung from the overhanging platform (port and starboard) on the aft deckhouse. Late in the war, in several ships extra lengths of hose were stored against the side of the aft deckhouse.

AFT DECK STOWAGE

WAIST BULWARK

Positioned in the bridge wings port and starboard were two or four sky lookout positions. Each mounting consisted of a simple tube support and seat. The binoculars were at eye level when the lookout was seated.

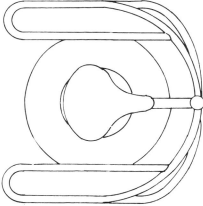

Sky Lookout Mounting

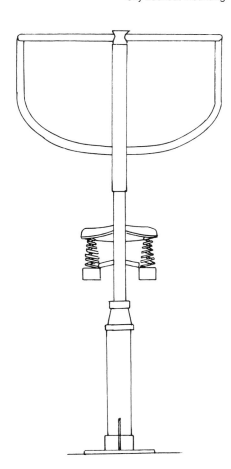

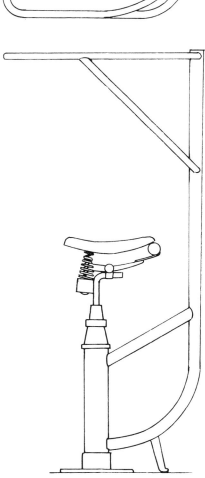

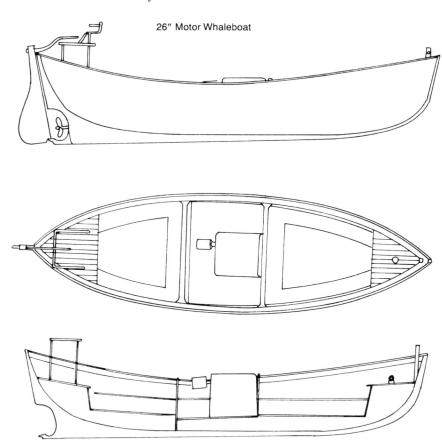

26″ Motor Whaleboat

Two whaleboats were carried by every ship throughout the war.

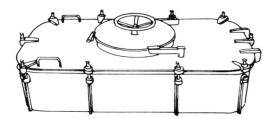

Hatchway Fitted on Foredeck & Fantail

Hose Reel

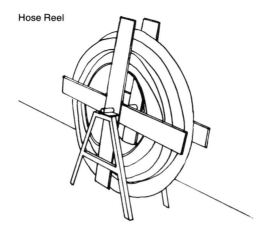

Boat Davits

FORE
DAVIT

26' Motor Whaleboat

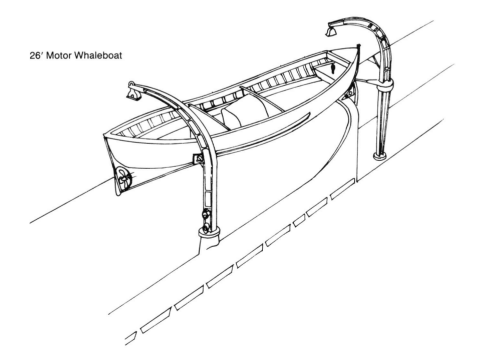

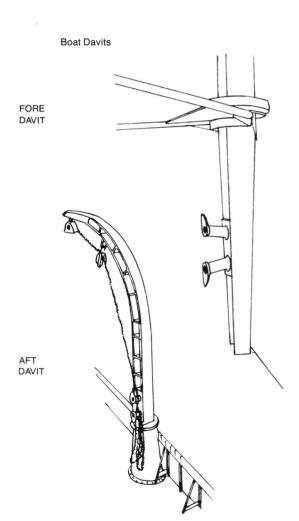

AFT
DAVIT

Cable Locker Covers on Foredeck

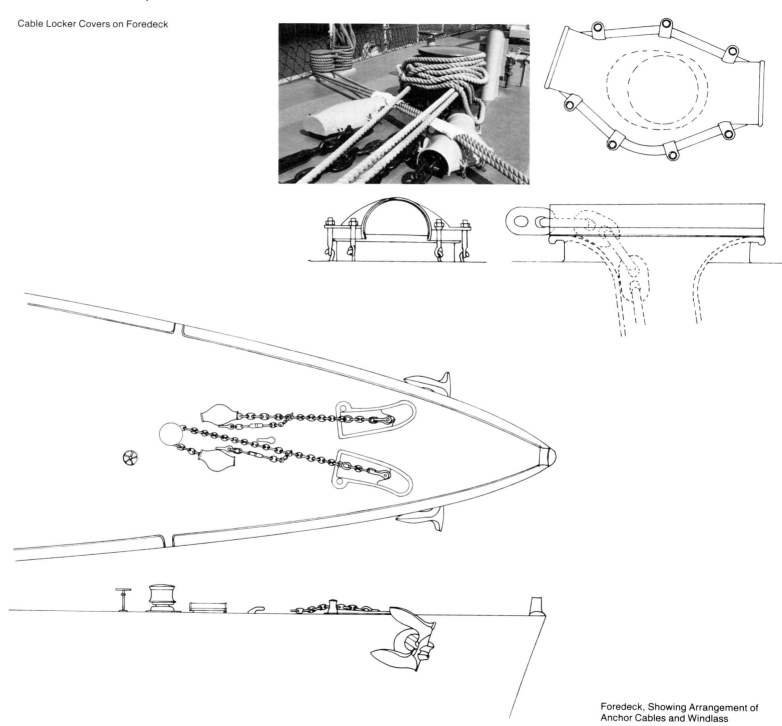

Foredeck, Showing Arrangement of
Anchor Cables and Windlass

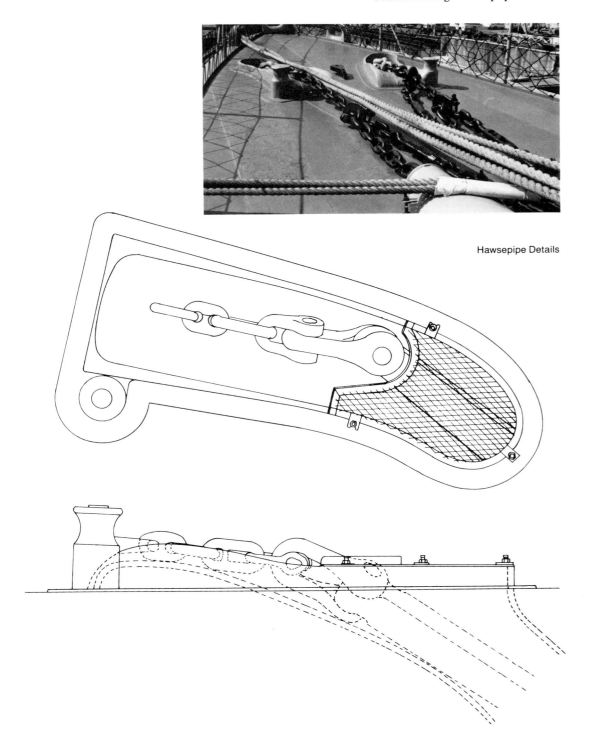

Hawsepipe Details

C. PROPELLERS, SHAFTING, AND RUDDERS

Details of Original Rudder

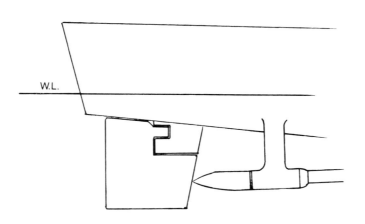

W.L.

Details of Rudder Fitted Postwar to
Many Fletchers to Increase
Maneuvering

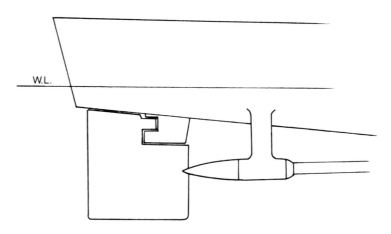

W.L.

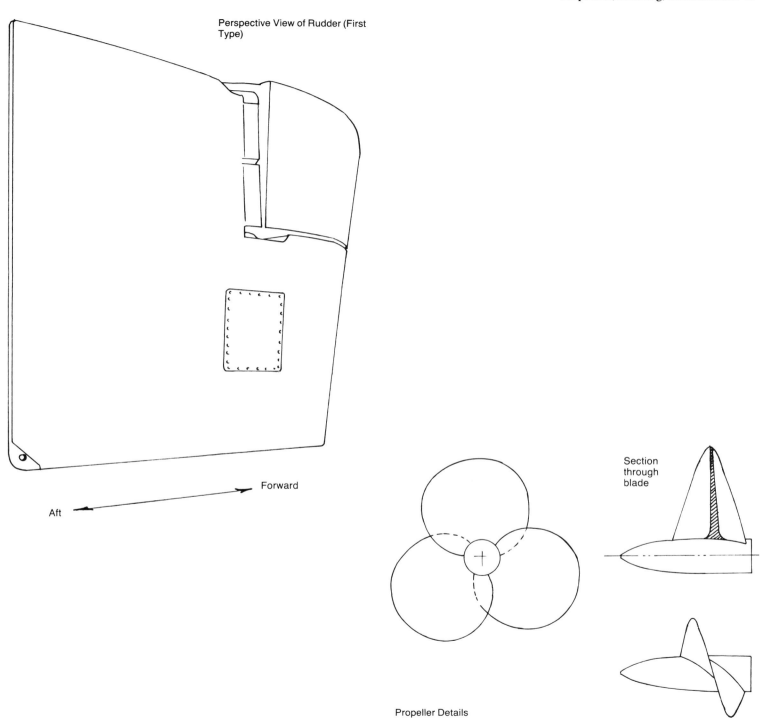

Perspective View of Rudder (First Type)

Forward

Aft

Section through blade

Propeller Details

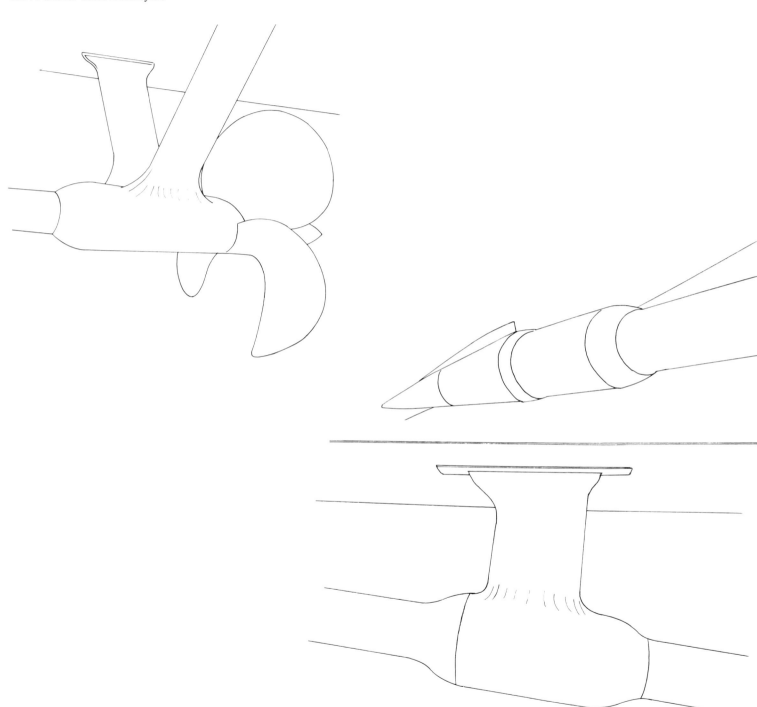

Propeller, Shafting, and Bracket Details

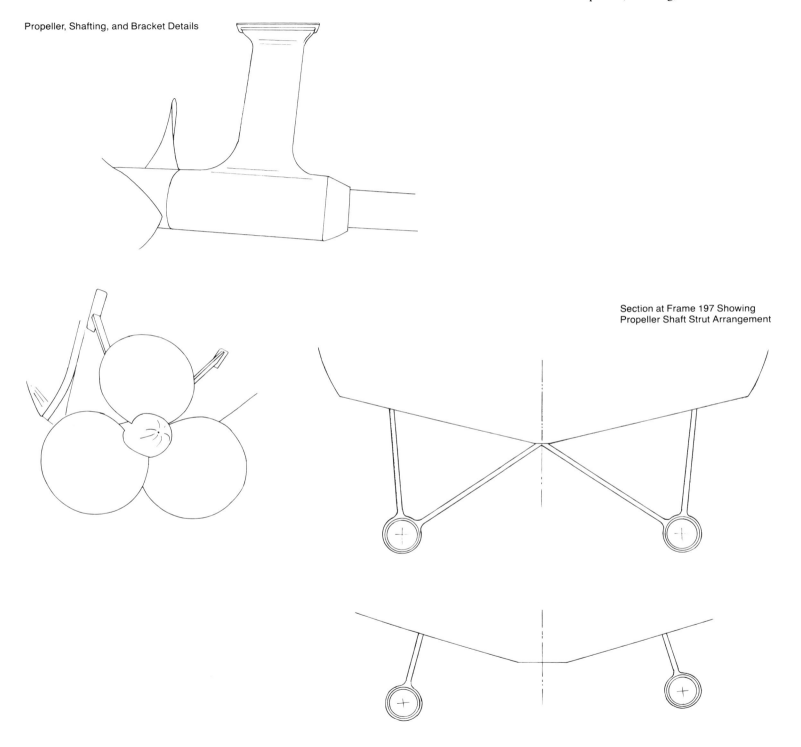

Section at Frame 197 Showing
Propeller Shaft Strut Arrangement

D. ANTENNAS

*Fletcher*s continued to serve into the sixties; seen here undergoing overhaul at Norfolk in February 1960 (from left to right) is the *Cassin Young, Cotten,* and *Dashiell. Cassin Young* was one of the few *Fletcher*s to be fitted with the SPS-28 air-search radar. Compare her rectangular antenna to the SPS-6C of the other vessels.

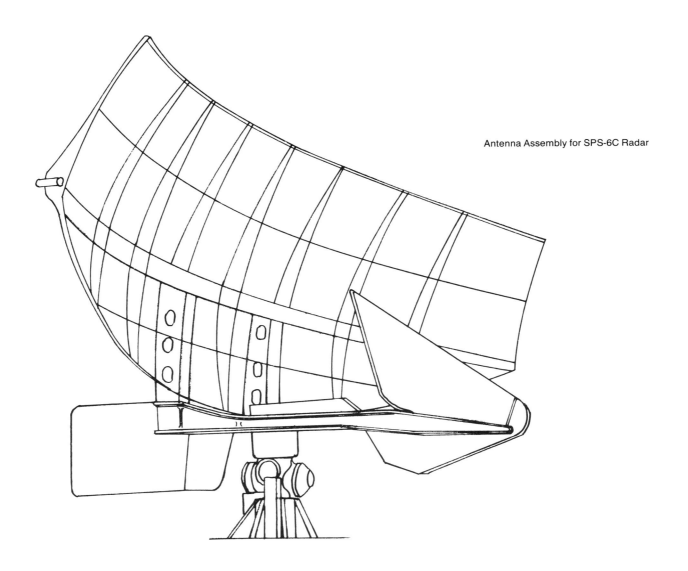

Antenna Assembly for SPS-6C Radar

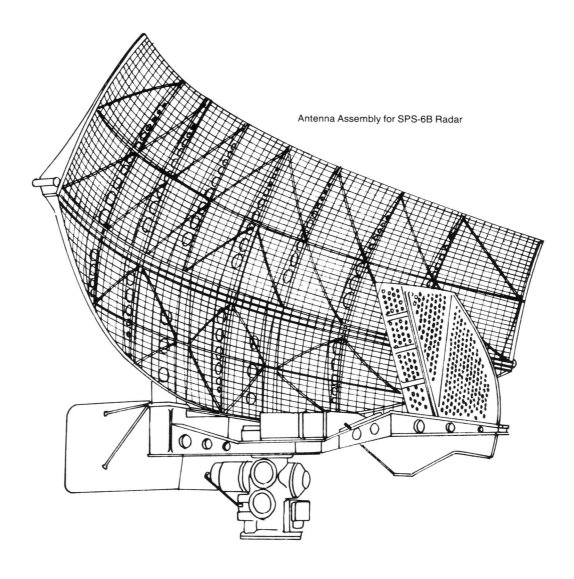

Antenna Assembly for SPS-6B Radar

Antenna Assembly for SU-2 Radar

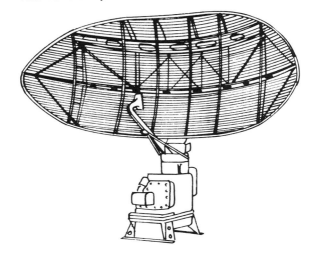

Antenna Assembly for SPS-10 Radar

Antenna Assembly for SC-4 Radar

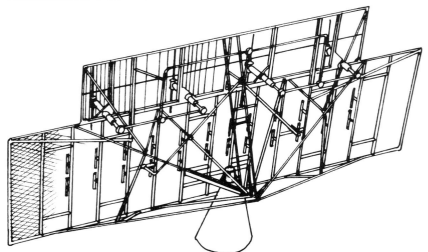

Antenna Assembly for SC-1 Radar

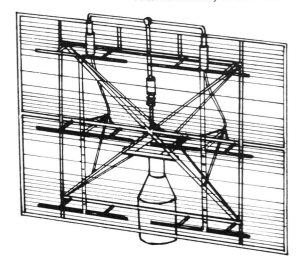

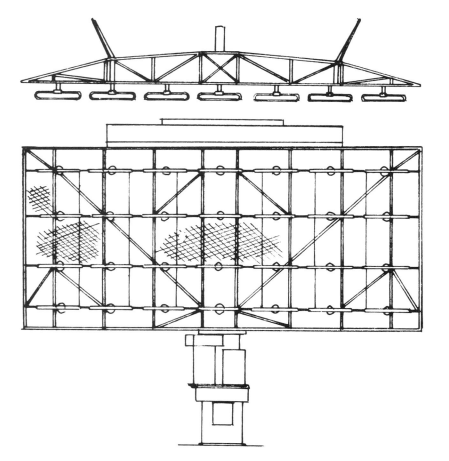

Antenna Assembly for SPS-17/28 Radar

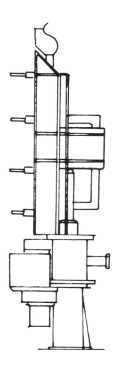

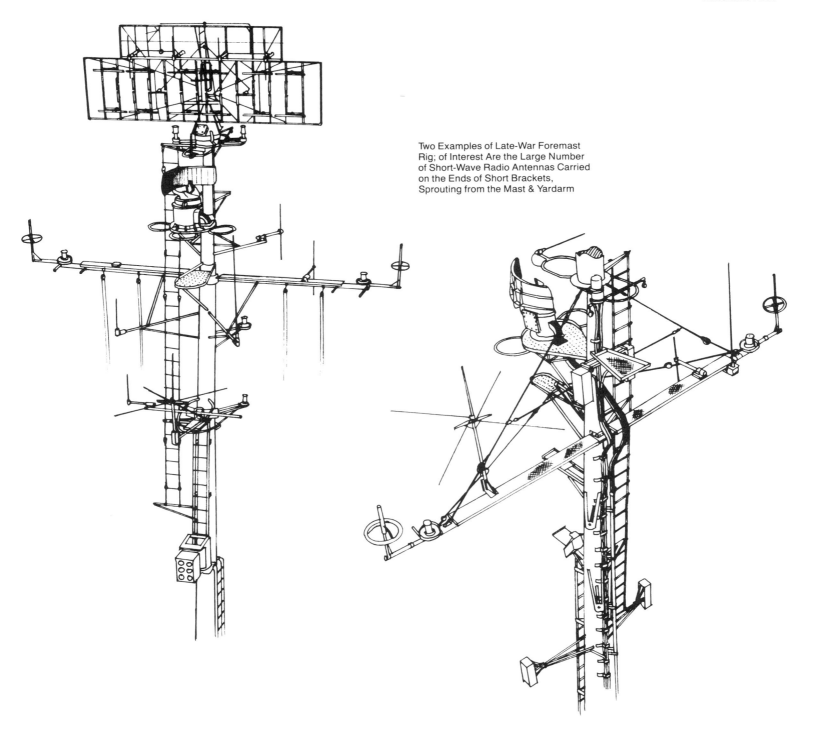

Two Examples of Late-War Foremast
Rig; of Interest Are the Large Number
of Short-Wave Radio Antennas Carried
on the Ends of Short Brackets,
Sprouting from the Mast & Yardarm

Foremast Showing Typical Field
Installation of ECM/ESM Gear Before
More Permanent Installation Using a
Mainmast Carried Aft

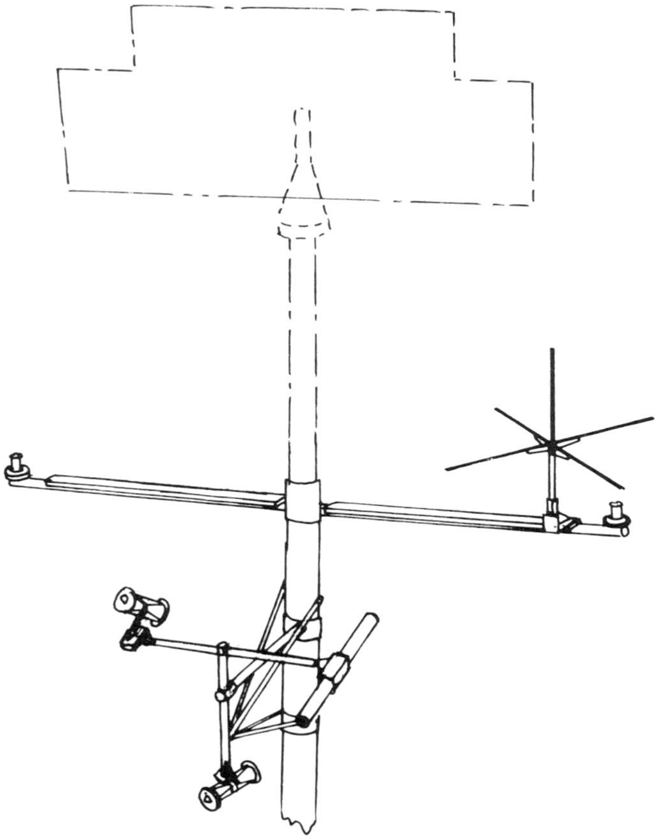

Countermeasures Receiving Antenna
AS-571/SLR as Fitted Postwar on
Mainmasts   49″   36″

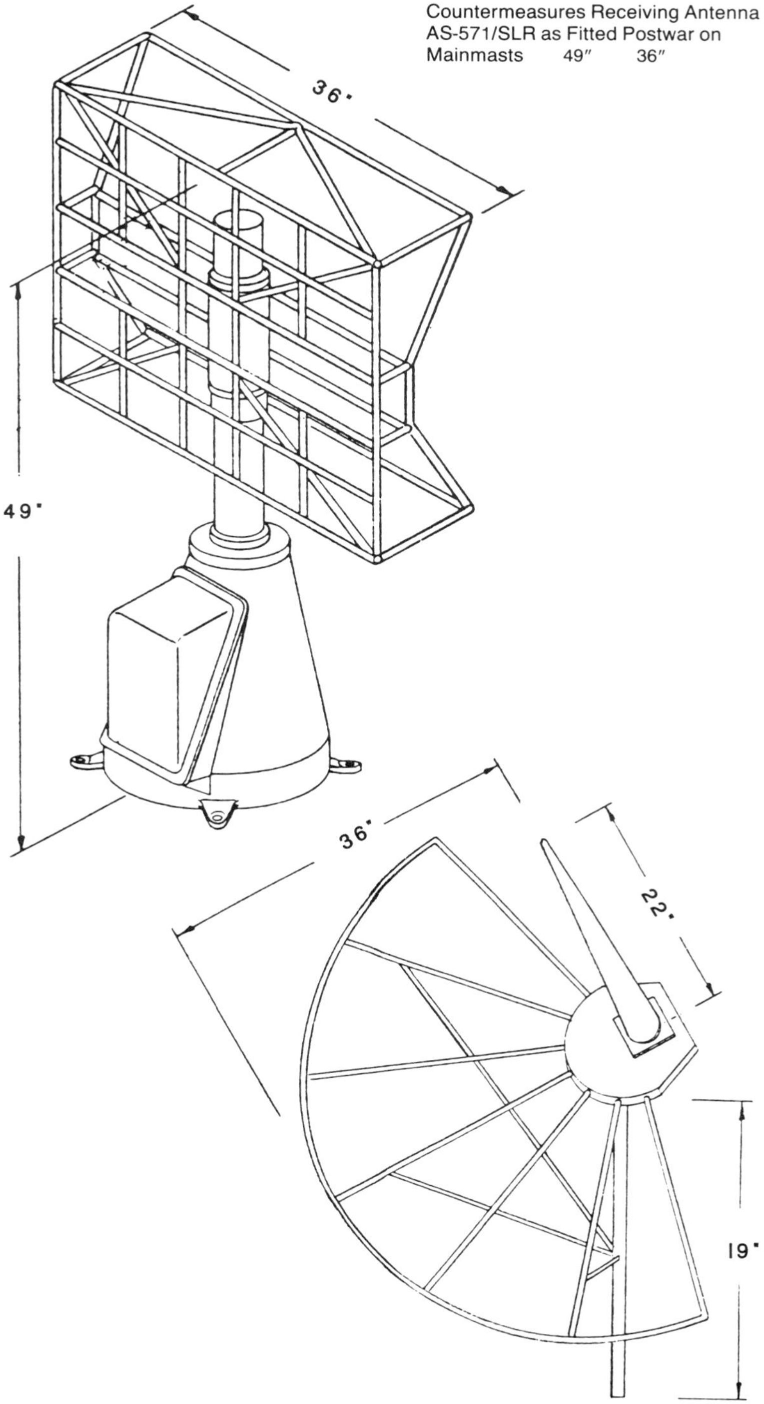

36°

49°

36°

22°

19°

Antenna Assembly for Direction
Finders DAQ & DAW

Antenna Assembly for Interception &
Jamming

Typical 1945 Mainmast Installation for
Interception & Jamming Equipment

1945 Main & Top Mast Arrangement for
Interception & Jamming Equipment

Antenna Assembly AS-390 for VHF
Radio Transmission—As Fitted to the *Jenkins*

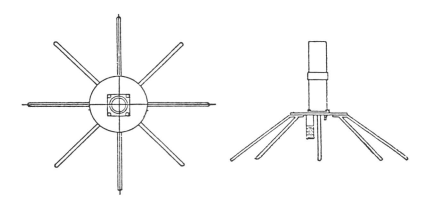

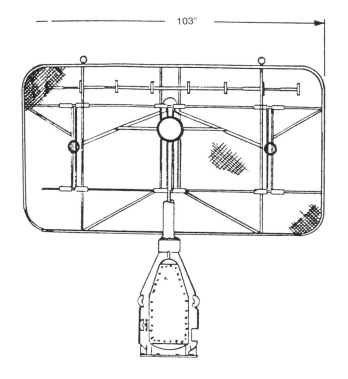

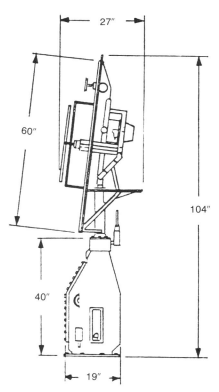

Antenna Assembly for SA Radar as
Fitted to the *Pringle* circa 1943

Omnidirectional Countermeasures
Receiving Antenna 66131

Antenna Assembly for SG-6 Radar

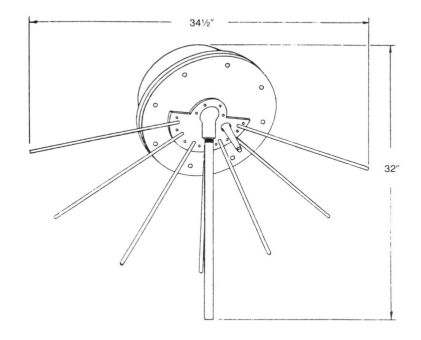

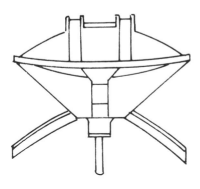

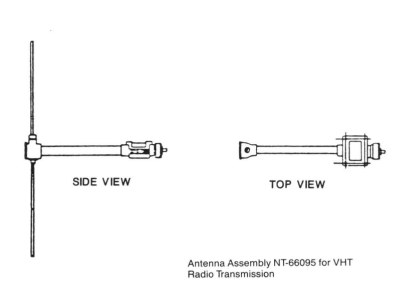

SIDE VIEW

TOP VIEW

Antenna Assembly NT-66095 for VHT
Radio Transmission

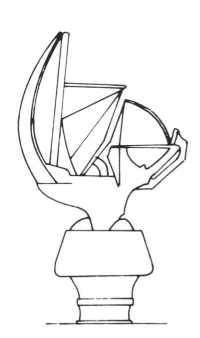

E. WEAPONS AND ASSOCIATED EQUIPMENT

5″ Mount Mk 30 Mod. 18/19—Carried
in Numbers Two, Three, & Four Positions.

5″ Mount Mk 30 Mod.30/31—Carried in
Numbers One & Five Positions

85° ELEVATION

DECK BLUE

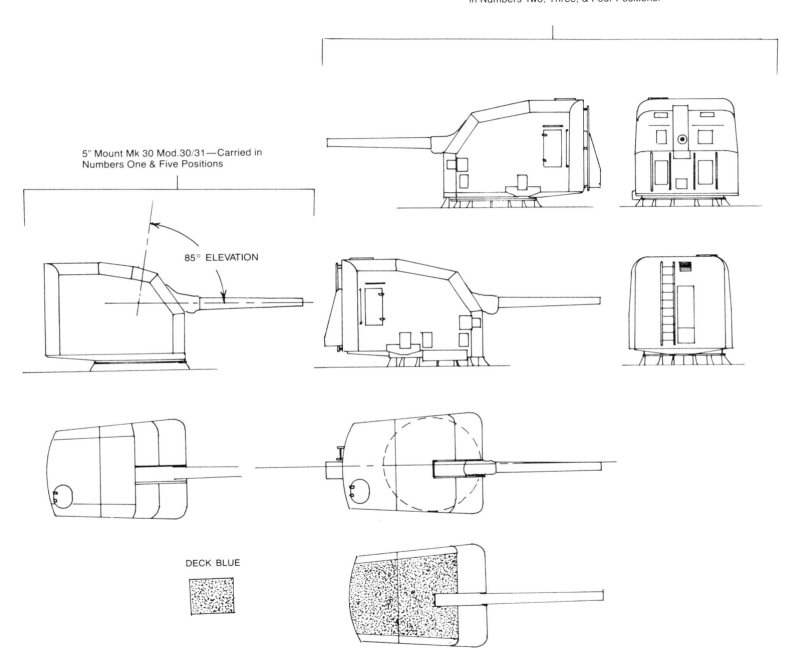

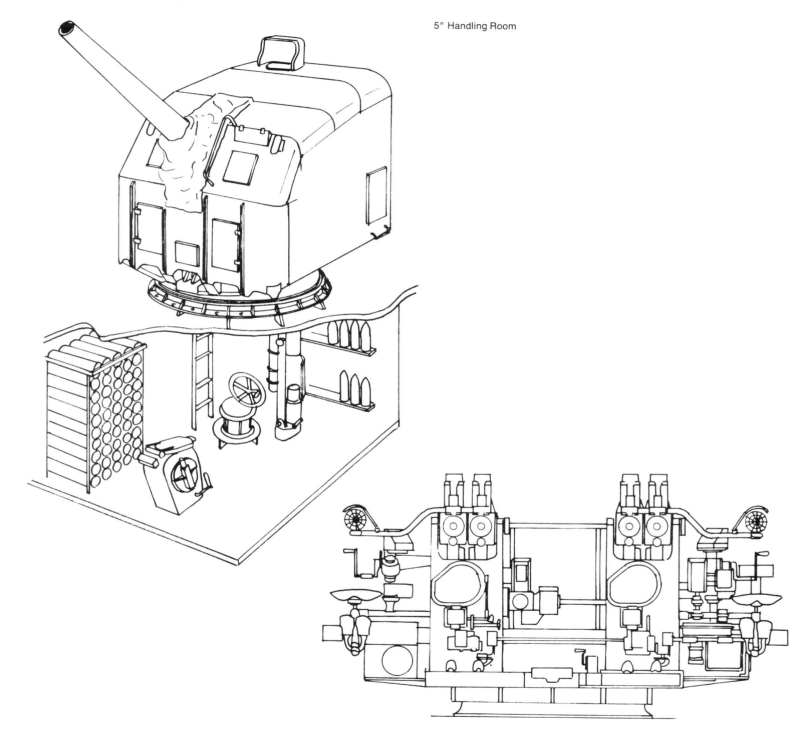

5″ Handling Room

Mk 4 Quadruple Bofors Mounting

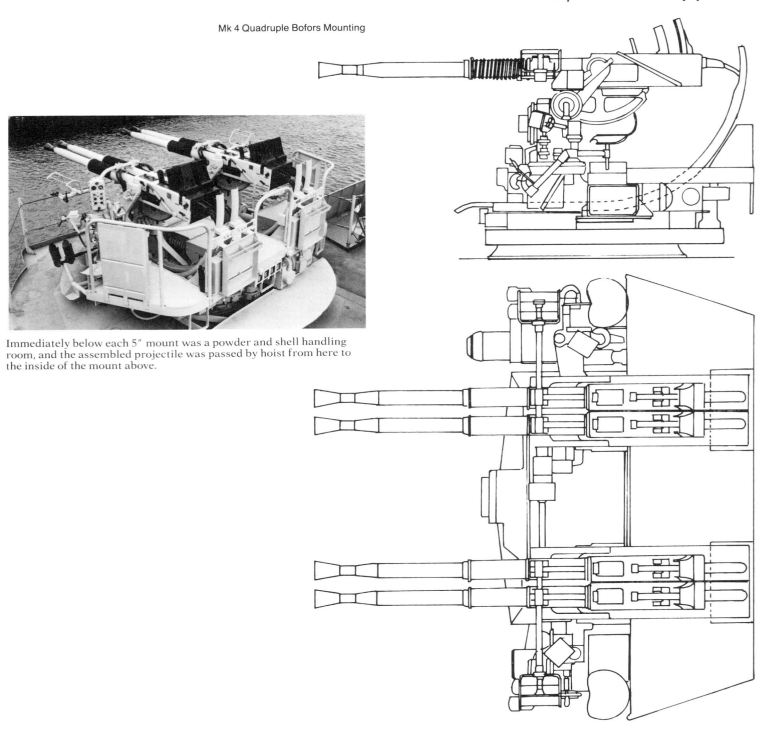

Immediately below each 5″ mount was a powder and shell handling room, and the assembled projectile was passed by hoist from here to the inside of the mount above.

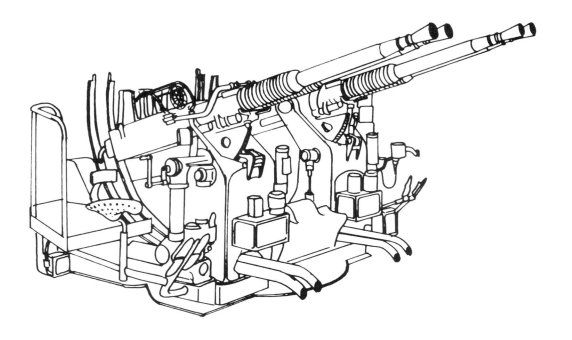

Mk 4 Quadruple Bofors Mounting

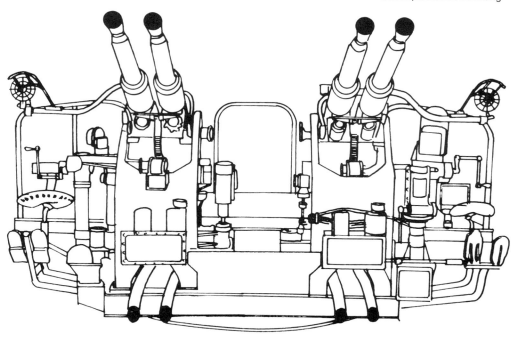

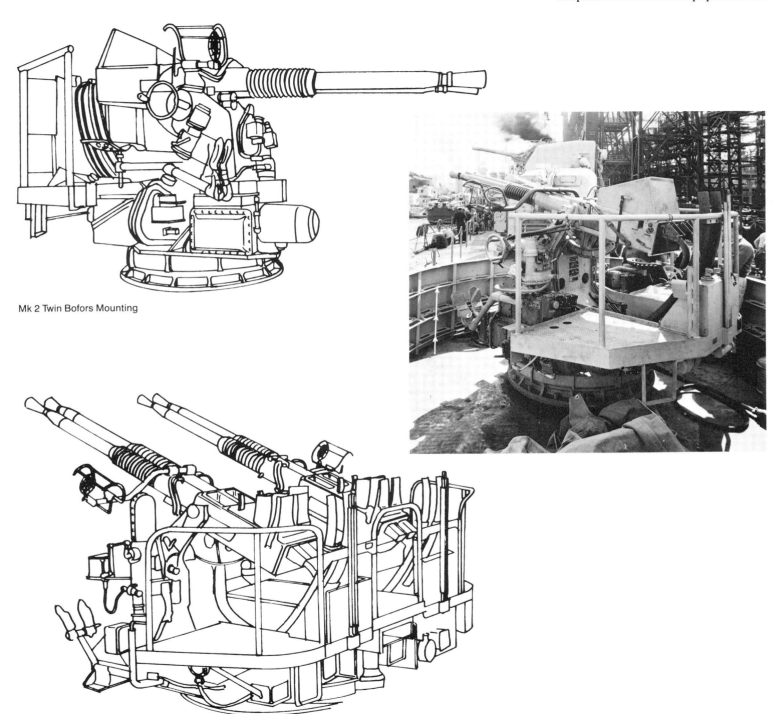

Mk 2 Twin Bofors Mounting

Mk 2 Twin Bofors Mounting

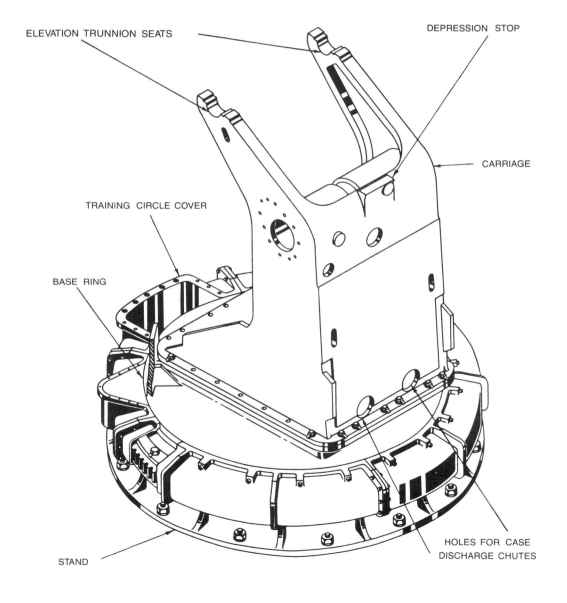

ELEVATION TRUNNION SEATS

DEPRESSION STOP

CARRIAGE

TRAINING CIRCLE COVER

BASE RING

HOLES FOR CASE DISCHARGE CHUTES

STAND

Mk 2 Twin Bofors Mounting

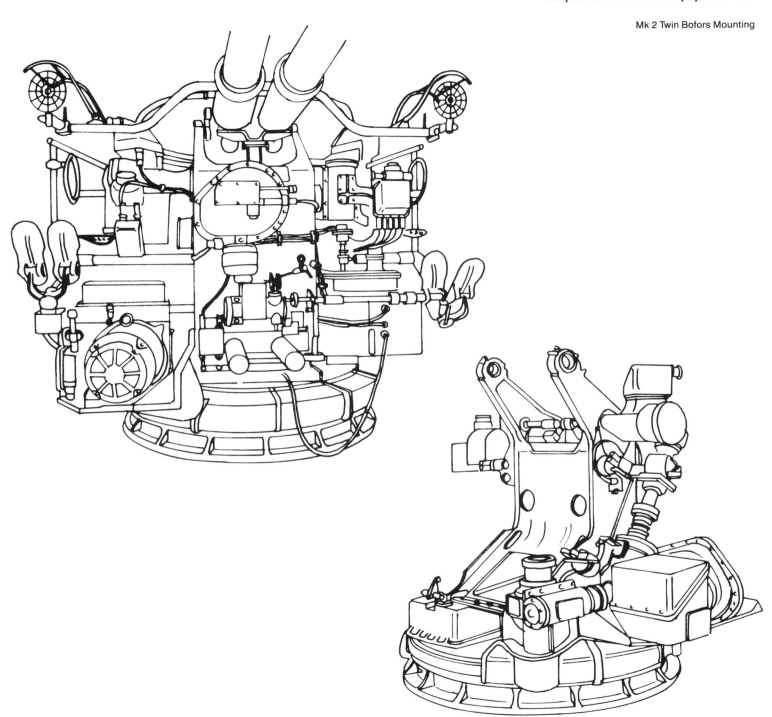

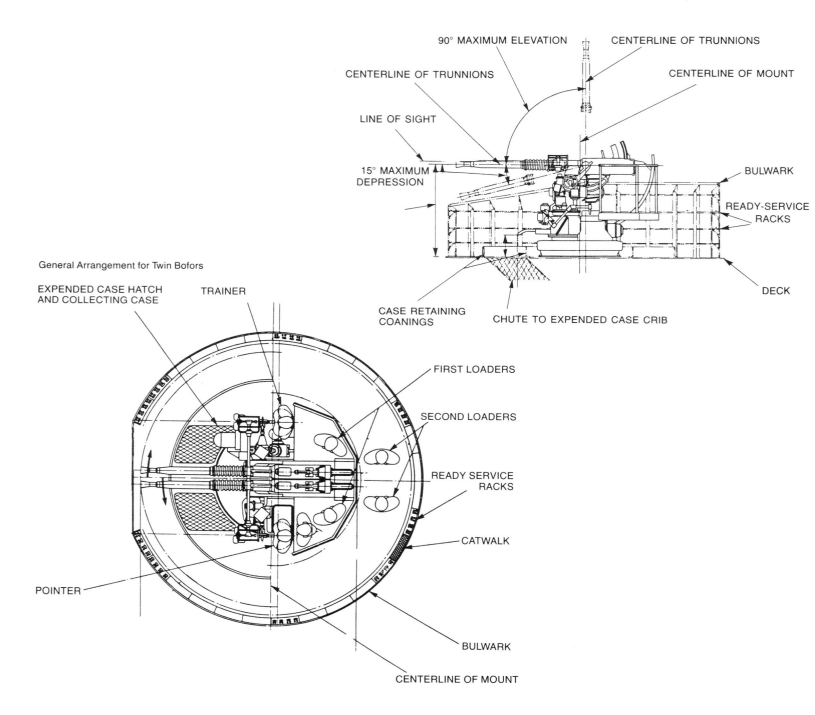

General Arrangement for Twin Bofors

90° MAXIMUM ELEVATION

CENTERLINE OF TRUNNIONS

CENTERLINE OF TRUNNIONS

CENTERLINE OF MOUNT

LINE OF SIGHT

15° MAXIMUM DEPRESSION

BULWARK

READY-SERVICE RACKS

DECK

CASE RETAINING COANINGS

CHUTE TO EXPENDED CASE CRIB

General Arrangement for Twin Bofors

EXPENDED CASE HATCH AND COLLECTING CASE

TRAINER

FIRST LOADERS

SECOND LOADERS

READY SERVICE RACKS

CATWALK

POINTER

BULWARK

CENTERLINE OF MOUNT

Almost ready to receive her 5-inch Bofors and 20-mm mountings is the *Cushing.* Photo taken at Bethlehem Steel Co., Staten Island Yard, on 8 October 1943.

Twin 3″ 50-Caliber Gun Mountings

The 3″ rapid-fire AA gun and mount was born out of a desperate 1945 need for a fast-firing gun with a heavy enough shell to blow apart the Japanese kamikaze. When the requirement was eventually fulfilled, these 3″ mounts (in the *Fletcher*s) replaced the waist and aft mounted Bofors.

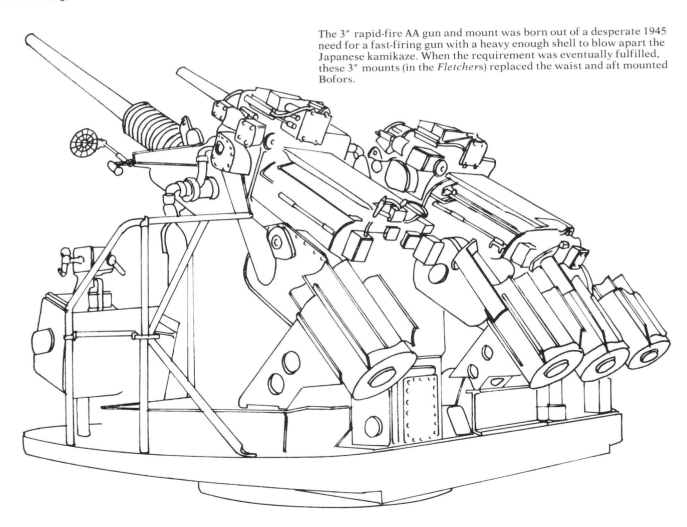

The *Waller* has just launched an ASW missile from her Mk 108; note the exhaust venting from the top rear of the turret. Photo was taken August 1959.

Waist view of the *O'Bannon* during final fitting out in mid-1942 immediately prior to delivery to the Navy.

Mk 108 ASW Rocket Launcher

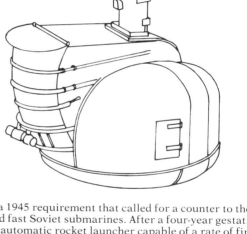

Conceived from a 1945 requirement that called for a counter to the expected new and fast Soviet submarines. After a four-year gestation, it emerged as an automatic rocket launcher capable of a rate of fire of 12 rounds per minute, with 22 rounds held in a ready-service magazine immediately beneath the launcher. The maximum range was almost 1,000 yards. First deliveries to the *Fletcher*s were made in the early fifties.

Single 20-mm Mounting

Twin 20-mm Mounting

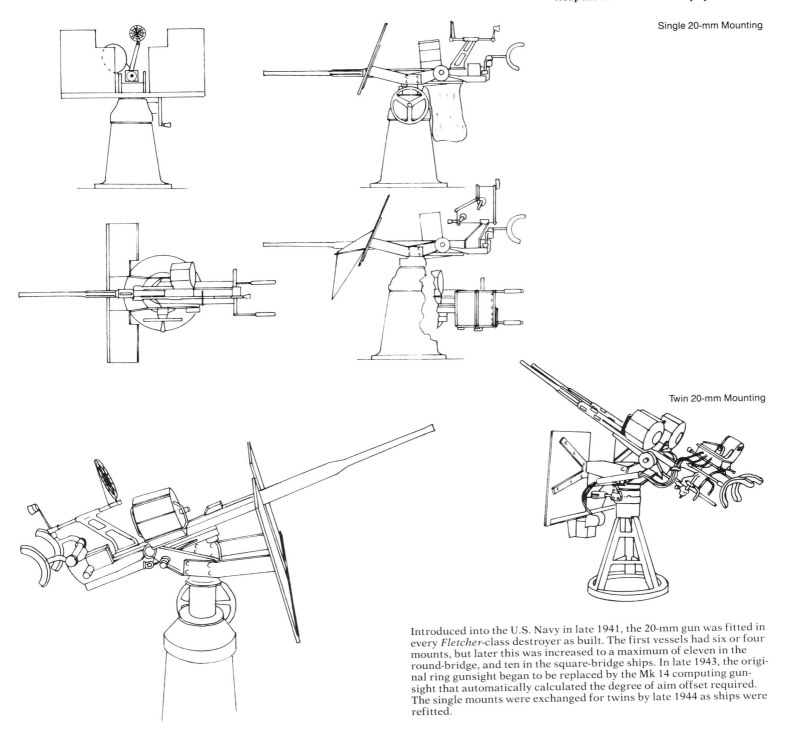

Introduced into the U.S. Navy in late 1941, the 20-mm gun was fitted in every *Fletcher*-class destroyer as built. The first vessels had six or four mounts, but later this was increased to a maximum of eleven in the round-bridge, and ten in the square-bridge ships. In late 1943, the original ring gunsight began to be replaced by the Mk 14 computing gunsight that automatically calculated the degree of aim offset required. The single mounts were exchanged for twins by late 1944 as ships were refitted.

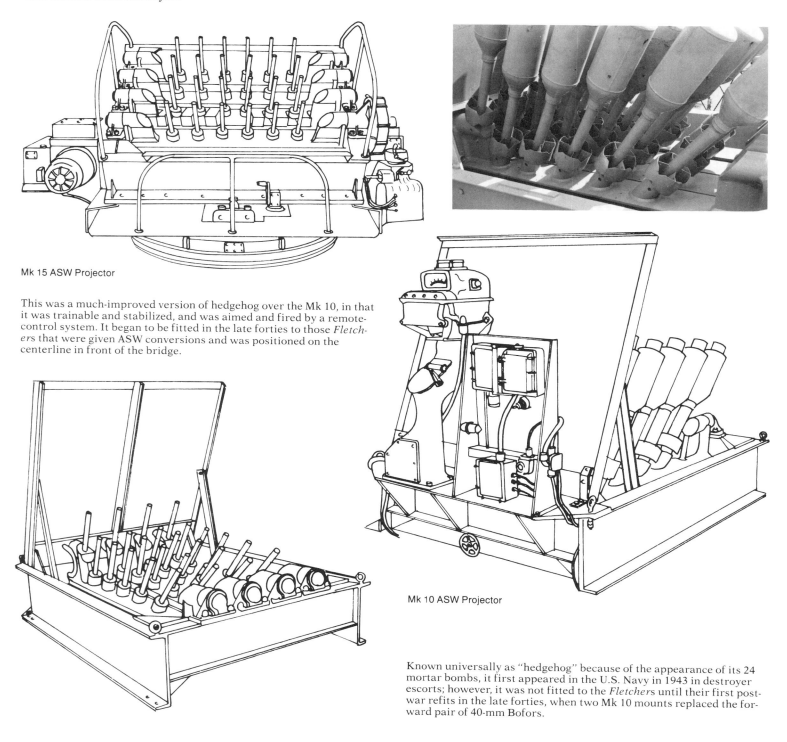

Mk 15 ASW Projector

This was a much-improved version of hedgehog over the Mk 10, in that it was trainable and stabilized, and was aimed and fired by a remote-control system. It began to be fitted in the late forties to those *Fletchers* that were given ASW conversions and was positioned on the centerline in front of the bridge.

Mk 10 ASW Projector

Known universally as "hedgehog" because of the appearance of its 24 mortar bombs, it first appeared in the U.S. Navy in 1943 in destroyer escorts; however, it was not fitted to the *Fletchers* until their first postwar refits in the late forties, when two Mk 10 mounts replaced the forward pair of 40-mm Bofors.

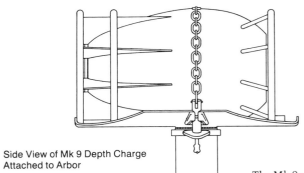

Side View of Mk 9 Depth Charge
Attached to Arbor

The Mk 9 was introduced as a faster sinking weapon and with a more stable trajectory than the earlier "ashcan"-shaped charge. It came into service in mid-1944, and by war's end was carried in all ships.

7.2" Mortar Bomb for Use with Mk 10 &
Mk 15 Projectors

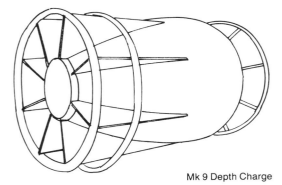

Mk 9 Depth Charge

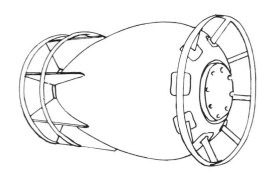

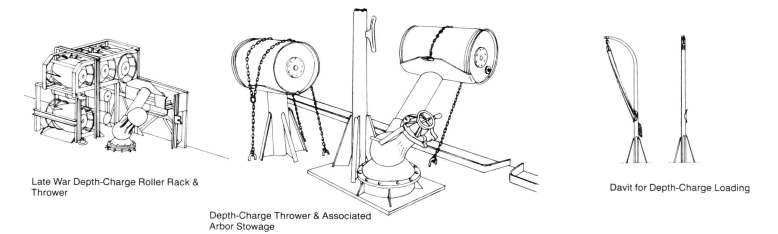

Late War Depth-Charge Roller Rack &
Thrower

Depth-Charge Thrower & Associated
Arbor Stowage

Davit for Depth-Charge Loading

Known as "K" guns, these throwers were used extensively; there were
six throwers (three per side) each one having four arbor charges alongside for quick reloading, with additional arbors stowed beside the
after deckhouse.

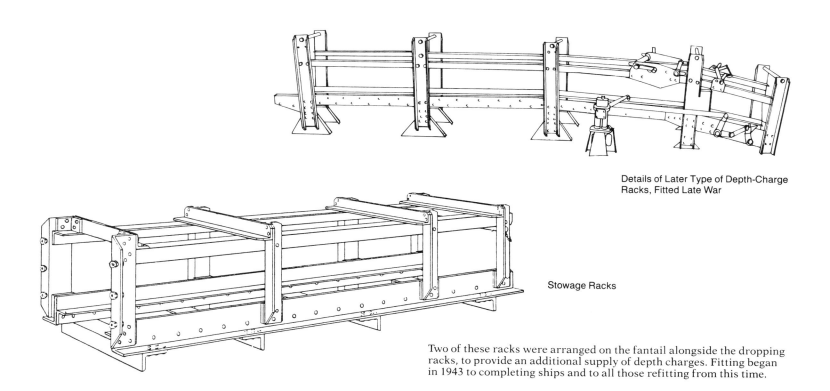

Details of Later Type of Depth-Charge
Racks, Fitted Late War

Stowage Racks

Two of these racks were arranged on the fantail alongside the dropping
racks, to provide an additional supply of depth charges. Fitting began
in 1943 to completing ships and to all those refitting from this time.

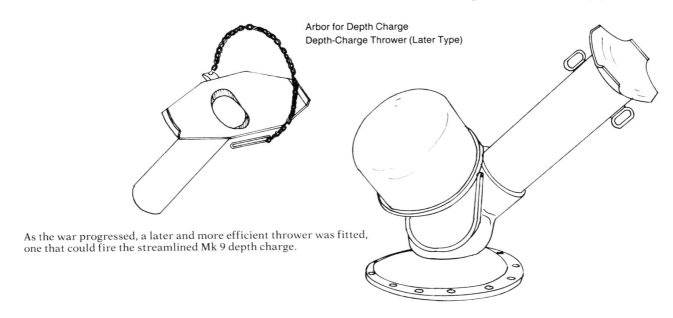

Arbor for Depth Charge
Depth-Charge Thrower (Later Type)

As the war progressed, a later and more efficient thrower was fitted, one that could fire the streamlined Mk 9 depth charge.

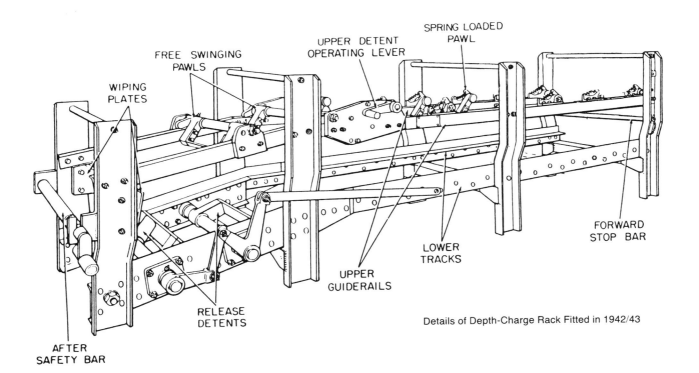

WIPING PLATES

FREE SWINGING PAWLS

UPPER DETENT OPERATING LEVER

SPRING LOADED PAWL

FORWARD STOP BAR

LOWER TRACKS

UPPER GUIDERAILS

RELEASE DETENTS

AFTER SAFETY BAR

Details of Depth-Charge Rack Fitted in 1942/43

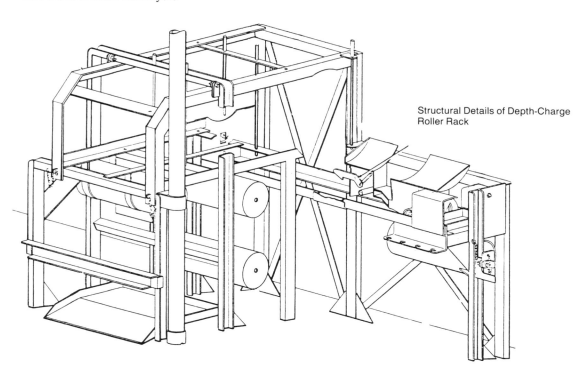

Structural Details of Depth-Charge
Roller Rack

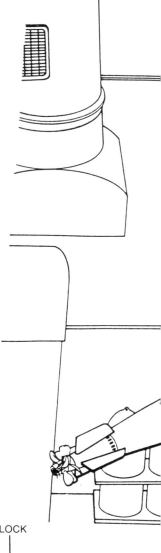

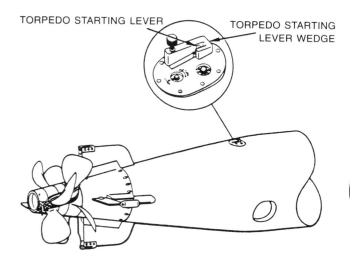

TORPEDO STARTING LEVER

TORPEDO STARTING
LEVER WEDGE

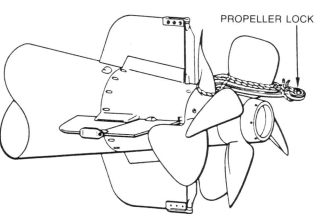

PROPELLER LOCK

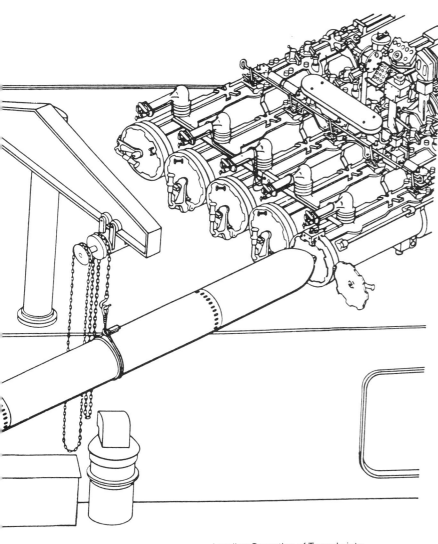

Loading Operation of Torpedo into
Torpedo Tube

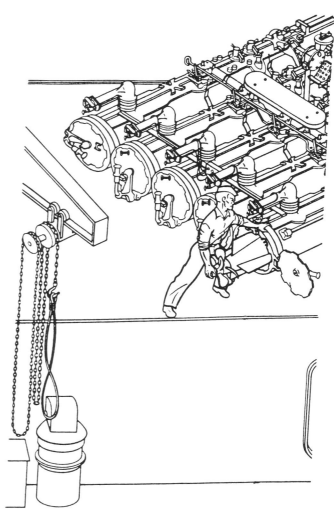

Details of Mk 14 & Mk 15 Quintuple
Torpedo Tubes

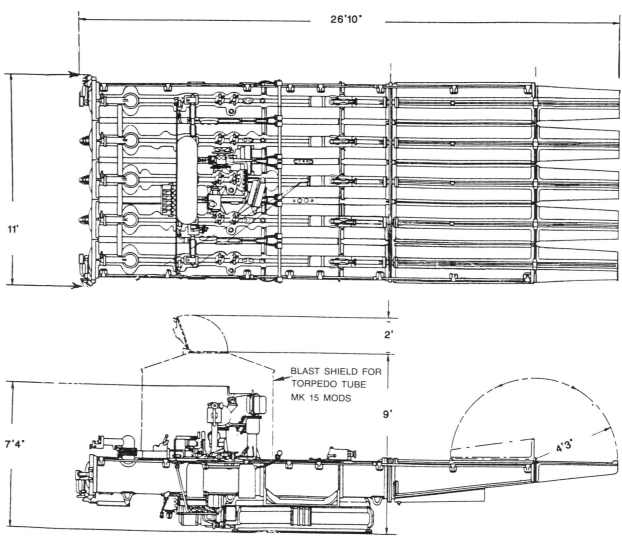

Looking aft along the waist of the *Radford* while undergoing her mid-1942 final fitting out at N.Y. Navy Yard.

On board the *Ringgold* in May 1943. Shown to good effect is the binnacle on the stack platform, and the Mk 14 torpedo tubes.

Torpedo Tube Assembly

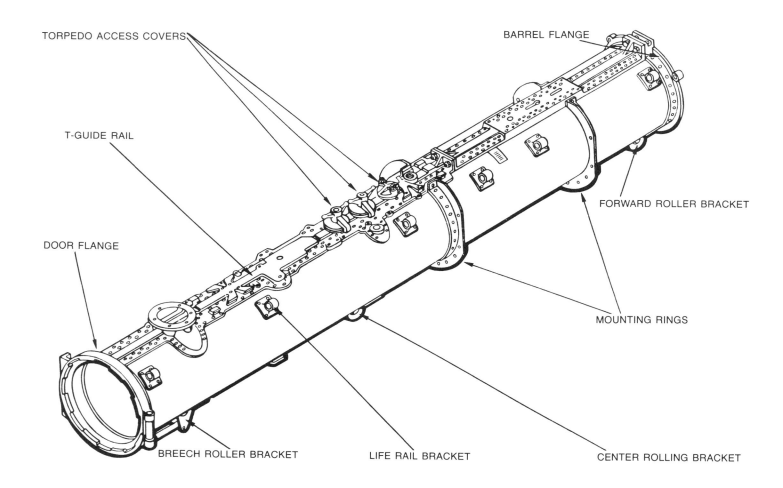

TORPEDO ACCESS COVERS

BARREL FLANGE

T-GUIDE RAIL

FORWARD ROLLER BRACKET

DOOR FLANGE

MOUNTING RINGS

BREECH ROLLER BRACKET

LIFE RAIL BRACKET

CENTER ROLLING BRACKET

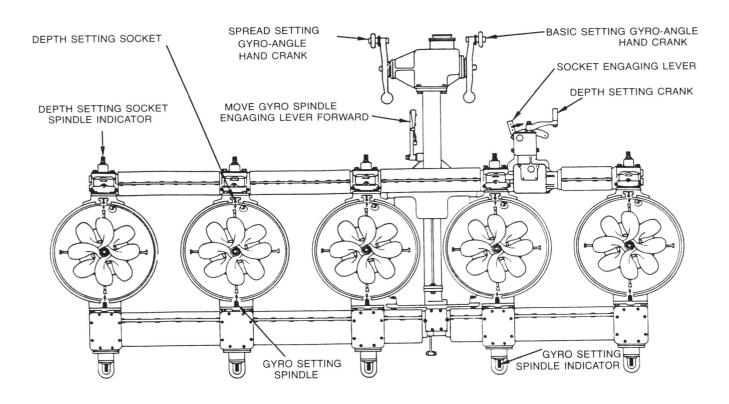

DEPTH SETTING SOCKET

SPREAD SETTING
GYRO-ANGLE
HAND CRANK

BASIC SETTING GYRO-ANGLE
HAND CRANK

DEPTH SETTING SOCKET
SPINDLE INDICATOR

MOVE GYRO SPINDLE
ENGAGING LEVER FORWARD

SOCKET ENGAGING LEVER

DEPTH SETTING CRANK

GYRO SETTING
SPINDLE

GYRO SETTING
SPINDLE INDICATOR

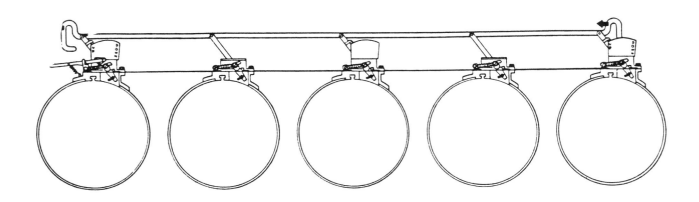

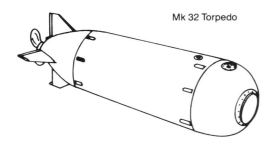

Mk 32 Torpedo

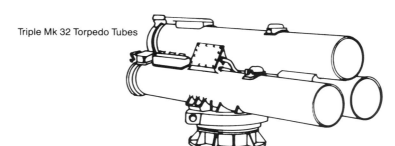

Triple Mk 32 Torpedo Tubes

A side-launched acoustic homing torpedo that was put into service in the early fifties. Because it was fitted with fins that had an overall width of over 25″, it could not be launched from the 21″ torpedo tubes already in service.

These were fitted after the war to many *Fletcher*s, when those ships had their 21″ quintuple mounts removed. Mks 44 and 46 homing torpedoes were carried in the Mk 32 tube.

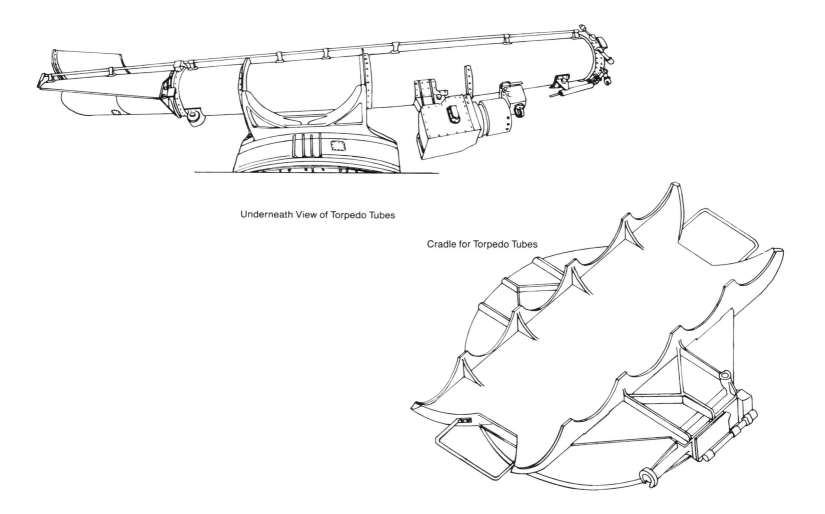

Underneath View of Torpedo Tubes

Cradle for Torpedo Tubes

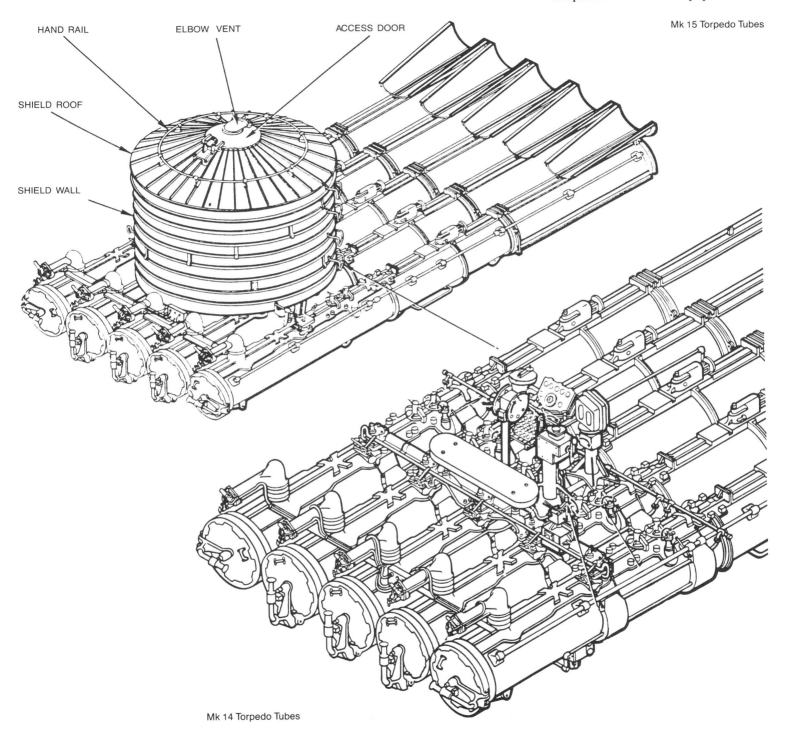

HAND RAIL

ELBOW VENT

ACCESS DOOR

SHIELD ROOF

SHIELD WALL

Mk 15 Torpedo Tubes

Mk 14 Torpedo Tubes

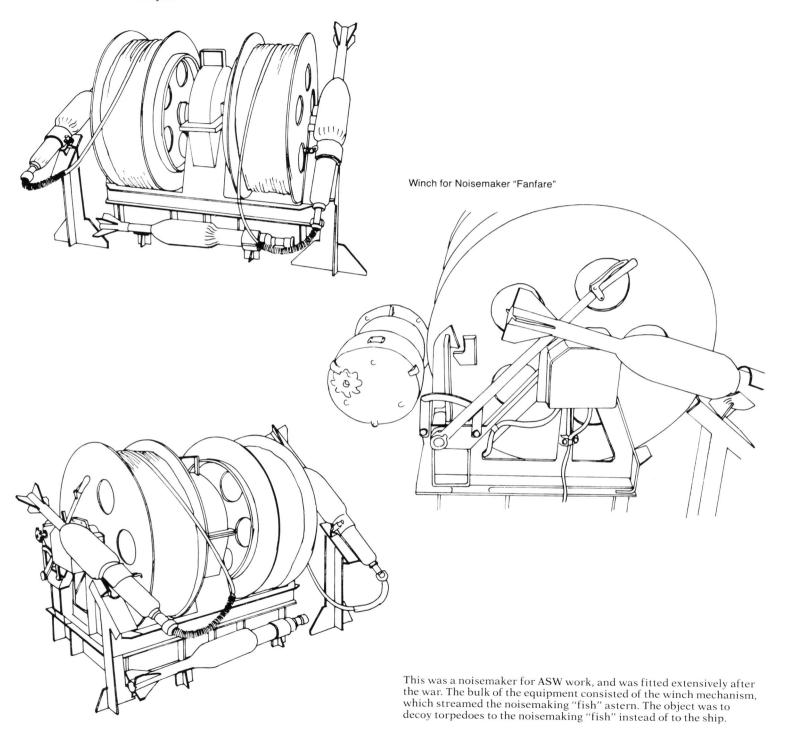

Winch for Noisemaker "Fanfare"

This was a noisemaker for ASW work, and was fitted extensively after the war. The bulk of the equipment consisted of the winch mechanism, which streamed the noisemaking "fish" astern. The object was to decoy torpedoes to the noisemaking "fish" instead of to the ship.

As the Mk 32 could not be launched from the normal torpedo tube, a dedicated launcher was developed in which the torpedo was laid in a cradle and the actual launching was achieved by the cradle arms raising the torpedo up and throwing it overboard.

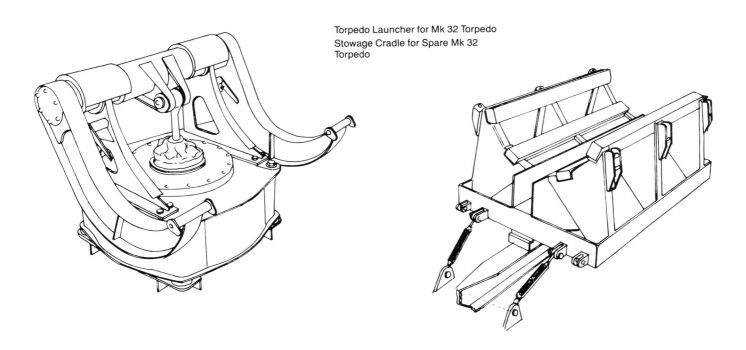

Torpedo Launcher for Mk 32 Torpedo

Stowage Cradle for Spare Mk 32 Torpedo

F. FIRE-CONTROL EQUIPMENT

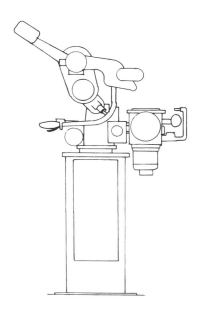

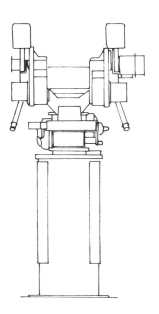

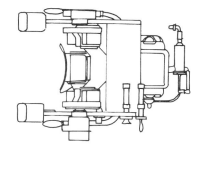

This was a manually operated lightweight piece of equipment, in essence a simple mount with a Mk 14 gunsight attached. Each Bofors mount had an associated Mk 51 director, and as the number of 40-mm mounts increased, so did the number of Mk 51 directors carried. For the midships Bofors, the Mk 51s were fitted around the aft stack, and for the forward Bofors, on the bridge roof, or with square-bridge vessels, in the bridge wings at the forward end.

Mk 51 40-mm Bofors Director

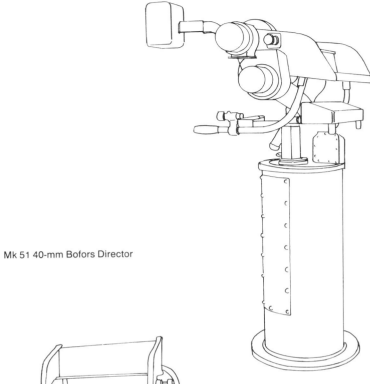

Mk 51 40-mm Bofors Director

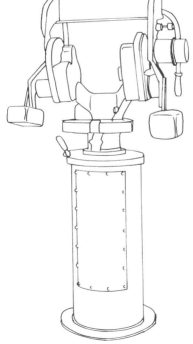

A good view of the Mk 49 director. This item was fitted to many *Fletcher*s in the 1943 period, but without the Mk 19 radar shown in the photo. By late 1944, these had been replaced by the better Mk 51 director.

Mk 37 Director with Mk 22/12 Radar
Assembly

The associated Mk 22 system was a height finder that used a parabolic antenna. Initially, it gave elevation data only, but a later modification also gave range data. Incorporated into the Mk 12 was an IFF (Identification Friend or Foe), the small parabolic antenna for which was sited in front of the two main troughs. As ships were refitted late in the war, the Mk 12/22 system replaced the earlier Mk 4, and by early 1945 this was accomplished in every vessel.

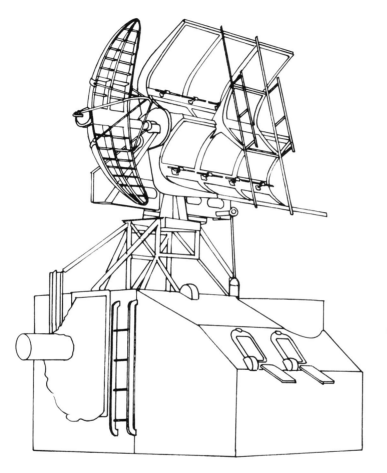

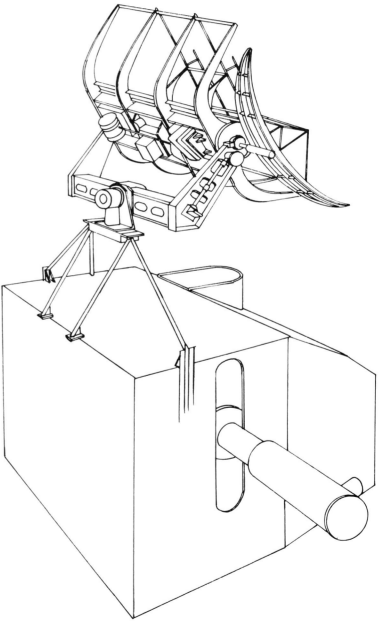

In early 1942, there began a program to develop a better gunnery radar system than the existing Mk 4. The result was the Mk 12, which reduced side lobes for a narrower radar beam with greater accuracy and greater resistance to countermeasures. The Mk 12 also had automatic range and rate tracking and in the later models, anti-jam features.

Mk 56 Director with Mk 35 Radar

This was designed as a dedicated radar-equipped fire director, for surface and air targets in all visibility conditions, for use on small ships. It was consequently fitted as the associated fire-control system for the postwar *Fletcher*s that had 3″ guns. Later versions of the Mk 56 had enclosed cockpits.

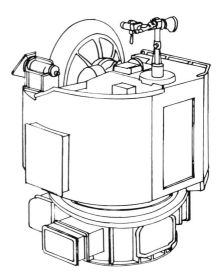

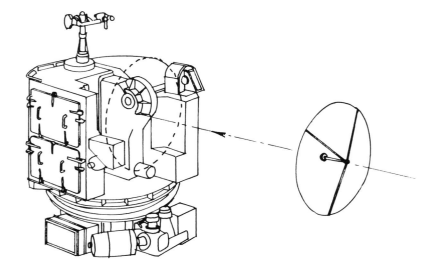

Mk 37 Director with Mk 4 Radar
Antenna

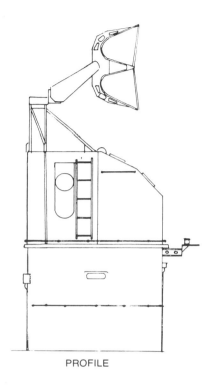

PROFILE

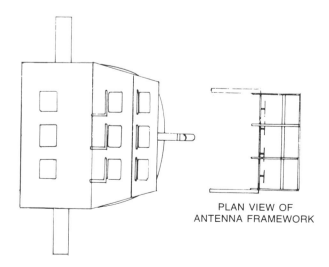

PLAN VIEW OF
ANTENNA FRAMEWORK

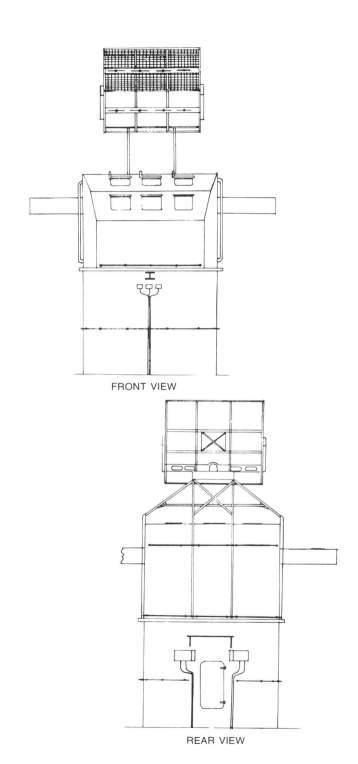

FRONT VIEW

REAR VIEW

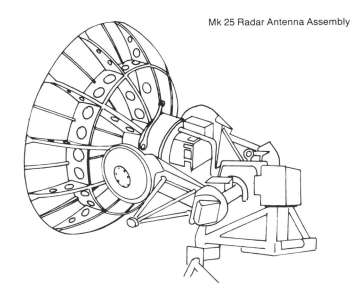

Mk 25 Radar Antenna Assembly

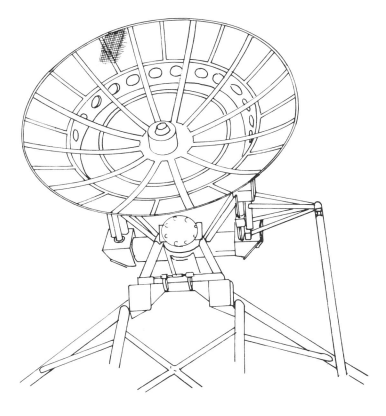

An X-band radar using a 4-foot parabolic dish antenna, fitted on the roof of the Mk 37 main gun director located above the bridge. The Mk 25 replaced the earlier Mk 4 and Mk 12/22 radars beginning early in the postwar period and eventually was fitted in all remaining active *Fletcher*s.

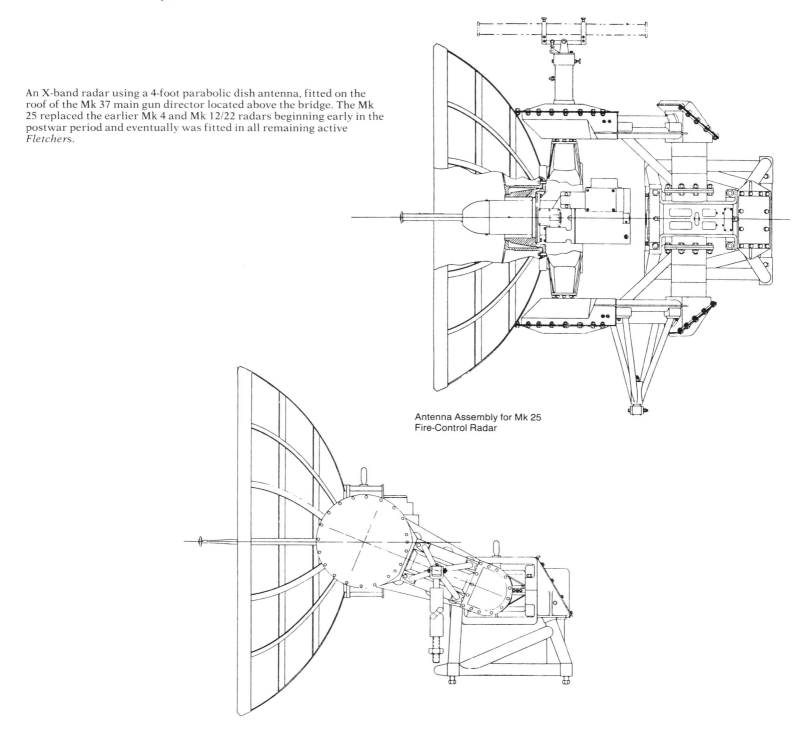

Antenna Assembly for Mk 25
Fire-Control Radar

Two of these were carried, one on each of the bridge wings, and were used to obtain bearings on enemy targets from lookout sightings.

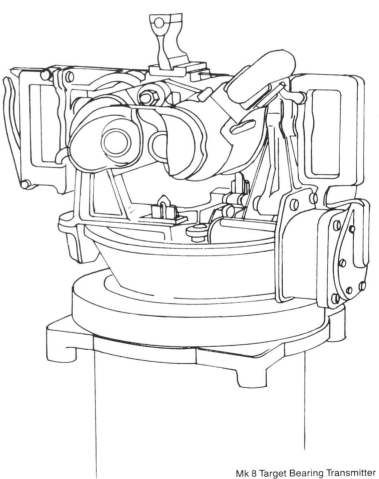

Mk 8 Target Bearing Transmitter

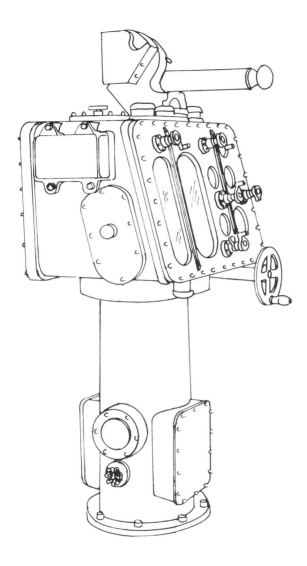

Torpedo Director

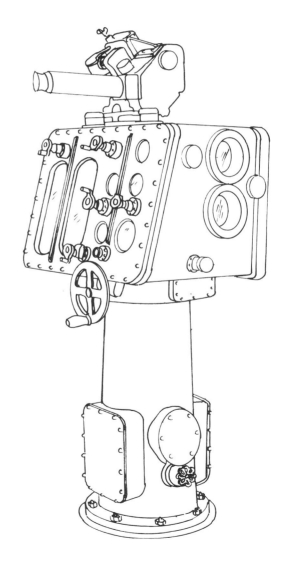

There were two of these fitted per ship, and as built, all ships carried them in the bridge wings, one to port, one to starboard.
In many of the ships that were given postwar refits, one director was removed, and the remaining one was moved to a centerline platform abaft the second stack.

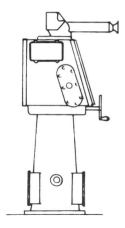
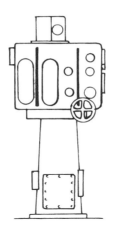
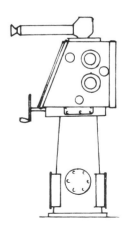

Torpedo Director

Looking down on the midship area of the *Miller* in August 1945. The Mk 35 radar aerials can easily be seen mounted in each of the quadruple Bofors. Note also the installation (made earlier) of the double depth-charge racks abreast the after deckhouse.

Beginning in mid-1945, several *Fletcher*s began to be fitted with two Mk 63 fire-control systems, each one located between the stacks to control the two waist quadruple 40-mm Bofors. The Mk 63 director was very similar in appearance to the Mk 52, but it worked in association with the Mk 34 radar fire-control system, the antenna assembly of which was mounted atop one pair of the quad Bofors gun barrels.

Mk 4 Quadruple Bofors Mounting Fitted with "On Mounting" Mk 34 Radar Assembly

G. CAMOUFLAGE AND FUNNEL DESIGNS

USS *LaVallette*—Camouflage Mid-1942

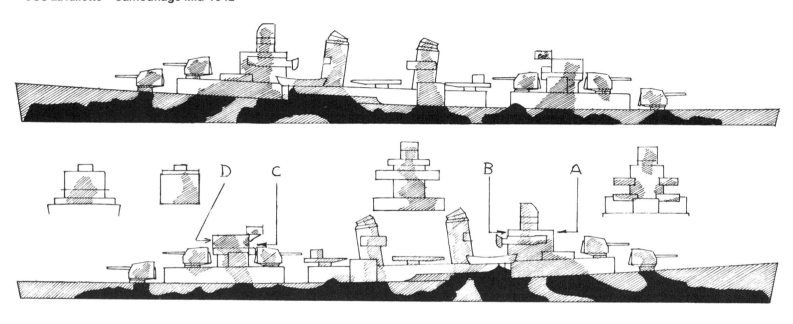

5 4 3 2 1

REAR VIEW OF 5″ TURRETS

NAVY BLUE

OCEAN GREY

HAZE GREY

ALL DECKS ARE DECK BLUE

5 4 3 2 1

FRONT VIEW OF 5″ TURRETS

USS *Yarnall*—Camouflage 1944

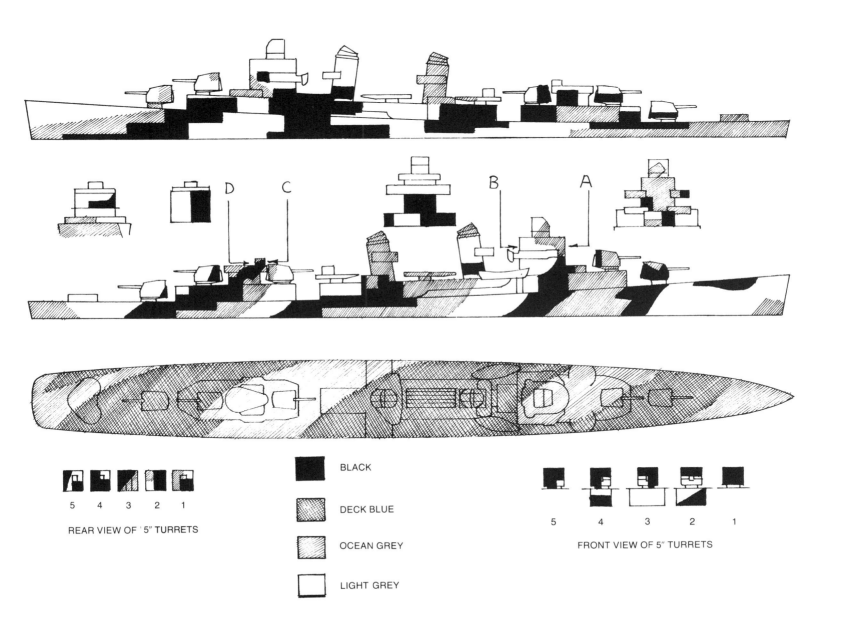

BLACK

DECK BLUE

OCEAN GREY

LIGHT GREY

5 4 3 2 1

REAR VIEW OF 5" TURRETS

5 4 3 2 1

FRONT VIEW OF 5" TURRETS

USS *Killen*—Camouflage 1944

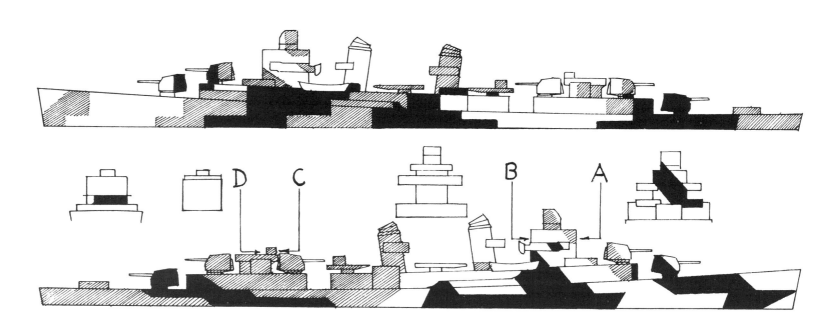

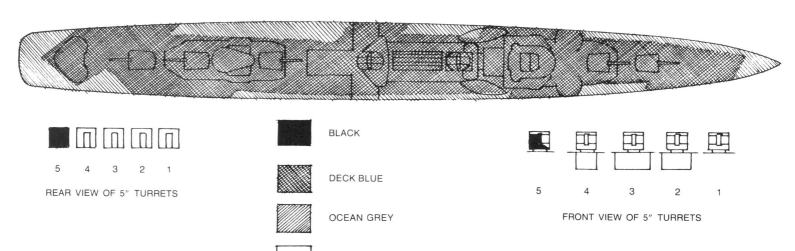

5   4   3   2   1

REAR VIEW OF 5″ TURRETS

■ BLACK

▨ DECK BLUE

▨ OCEAN GREY

□ HAZE GREY

5   4   3   2   1

FRONT VIEW OF 5″ TURRETS

USS *Heermann*—Camouflage 1944

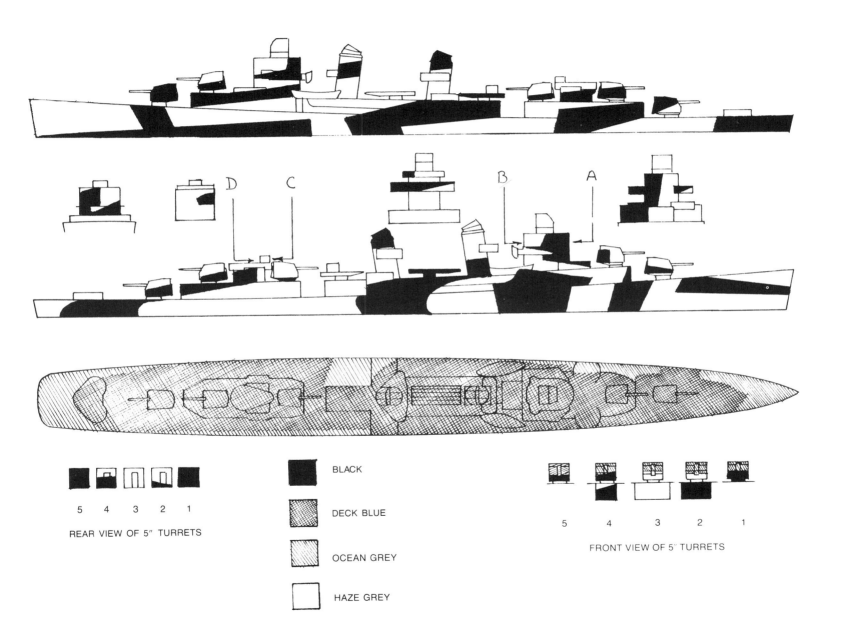

REAR VIEW OF 5" TURRETS

5 4 3 2 1

BLACK

DECK BLUE

OCEAN GREY

HAZE GREY

FRONT VIEW OF 5" TURRETS

5 4 3 2 1

Funnel Designs

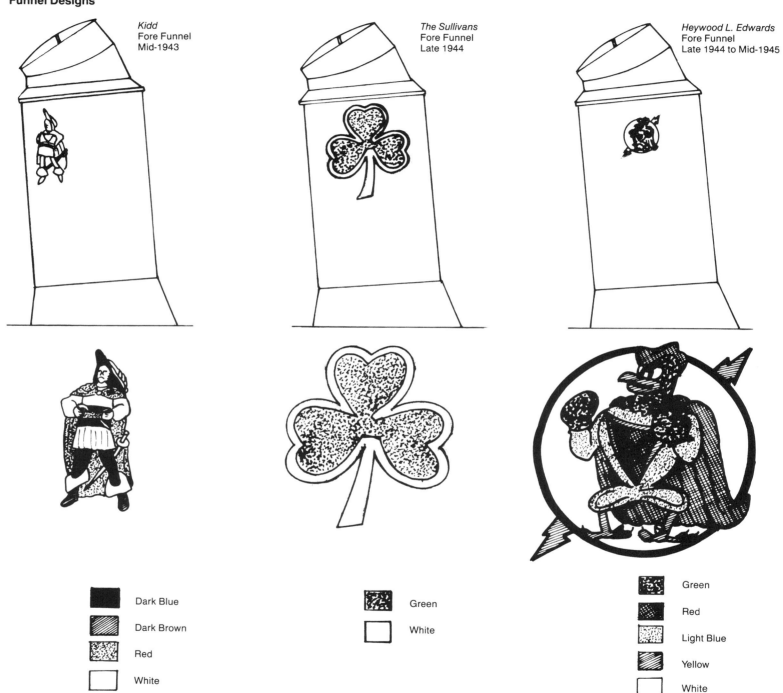

Kidd
Fore Funnel
Mid-1943

The Sullivans
Fore Funnel
Late 1944

Heywood L. Edwards
Fore Funnel
Late 1944 to Mid-1945

Dark Blue

Dark Brown

Red

White

Green

White

Green

Red

Light Blue

Yellow

White

Mertz
Fore Funnel
August 1945

Cassin Young
Aft Funnel
Mid-1945

Name Unknown
Aft Funnel
April 1945

Red

Colors Unknown

Black

White

List of Ships

Name/Builder	Laid Down	Commissioned	Name/Builder	Laid Down	Commissioned
445 *Fletcher*/Fed	2 Oct 41	30 Jun 42	498 *Philip*/Fed	7 May 42	21 Nov 42
446 *Radford*/Fed	2 Oct 41	22 Jul 42	499 *Renshaw*/Fed	7 May 42	5 Dec 42
447 *Jenkins*/Fed	27 Nov 41	31 Jul 42	500 *Ringgold*/Fed	25 Jun 42	30 Dec 42
448 *LaVallette*/Fed	27 Nov 41	12 Aug 42	501 *Schroeder*/Fed	25 Jun 42	1 Jan 43
449 *Nicholas*/Bath	3 Mar 41	4 Jun 42	502 *Sigsbee*/Fed	22 Jul 42	23 Jan 43
450 *O'Bannon*/Bath	3 Mar 41	26 Jun 42	507 *Conway*/Bath	5 Nov 41	9 Oct 42
451 *Chevalier*/Bath	30 Apr 41	20 Jul 42	508 *Cony*/Bath	24 Dec 41	30 Oct 42
465 *Saufley*/Fed	27 Jan 42	9 Aug 42	509 *Converse*/Bath	23 Feb 42	20 Nov 42
466 *Waller*/Fed	12 Feb 42	1 Oct 42	510 *Eaton*/Bath	17 Mar 42	4 Dec 42
467 *Strong*/Bath	30 Apr 41	7 Aug 42	511 *Foote*/Bath	14 Apr 42	22 Dec 42
468 *Taylor*/Bath	28 Aug 41	28 Aug 42	512 *Spence*/Bath	18 May 42	8 Jan 43
469 *De Haven*/Bath	27 Sep 41	21 Sep 42	513 *Terry*/Bath	8 Jun 42	27 Jan 43
470 *Bache*/BethSI	19 Nov 41	14 Nov 42	514 *Thatcher*/Bath	29 Jun 42	10 Feb 43
471 *Beale*/BethSI	19 Dec 41	23 Dec 42	515 *Anthony*/Bath	17 Aug 42	26 Feb 43
472 *Guest*/BosNY	27 Sep 41	15 Dec 42	516 *Wadsworth*/Bath	18 Aug 42	16 Mar 43
473 *Bennett*/BosNY	10 Dec 41	9 Feb 43	517 *Walker*/Bath	31 Aug 42	3 Apr 43
474 *Fullam*/BosNY	10 Dec 41	9 Feb 43	518 *Brownson*/BethSI	15 Feb 42	3 Feb 43
475 *Hudson*/BosNY	20 Feb 42	13 Apr 43	519 *Daly*/BethSI	29 Apr 42	10 Mar 43
476 *Hutchins*/BosNY	27 Sep 41	17 Nov 42	520 *Isherwood*/BethSI	12 May 42	12 Apr 43
477 *Pringle*/CharNY	31 Jul 41	15 Sep 42	521 *Kimberly*/BethSI	27 Jul 42	22 May 43
478 *Stanly*/CharNY	15 Sep 41	15 Oct 42	522 *Luce*/BethSI	24 Aug 42	21 Jun 43
479 *Stevens*/CharNY	30 Dec 41	1 Feb 43	526 *Abner Read*/BethSF	30 Oct 41	5 Feb 43
480 *Halford*/PSNY	3 Jun 41	10 Apr 43	527 *Ammen*/BethSF	29 Nov 41	12 Mar 43
481 *Leutze*/PSNY	3 Jun 41	4 Mar 44	528 *Mullany*/BethSF	15 Jan 42	10 May 43

Name/Builder	Laid Down	Commissioned	Name/Builder	Laid Down	Commissioned
529 *Bush*/BethSF	12 Feb 42	10 May 43	578 *Wickes*/Orange	15 Apr 42	16 Jun 43
530 *Trathen*/BethSF	18 Jul 42	28 May 43	579 *William D. Porter*/Orange	7 May 42	6 Jul 43
531 *Hazelwood*/BethSF	11 Apr 42	18 Jun 43	580 *Young*/Orange	7 May 42	31 Jul 43
532 *Heermann*/BethSF	8 May 42	6 Jul 43	581 *Charrette*/BosNY	20 Feb 42	18 May 43
533 *Hoel*/BethSF	4 Jun 42	29 Jul 43	582 *Conner*/BosNY	16 Apr 42	8 Jun 43
534 *McCord*/BethSF	17 Mar 42	19 Aug 43	583 *Hall*/BosNY	16 Apr 42	6 Jul 43
535 *Miller*/BethSF	18 Aug 42	31 Aug 43	584 *Halligan*/BosNY	9 Nov 42	19 Aug 43
536 *Owen*/BethSF	17 Sep 42	20 Sep 43	585 *Haraden*/BosNY	9 Nov 42	16 Sep 43
537 *The Sullivans*/BethSF	10 Oct 42	30 Sep 43	586 *Newcomb*/BosNY	19 Mar 43	10 Nov 43
538 *Stephen Potter*/BethSF	27 Oct 42	21 Oct 43	587 *Bell*/CharNY	30 Dec 41	4 Mar 43
539 *Tingey*/BethSF	22 Oct 42	25 Nov 43	588 *Burns*/CharNY	9 May 42	3 Apr 43
540 *Twining*/BethSF	20 Nov 42	1 Dec 43	589 *Izard*/CharNY	9 May 42	15 May 43
541 *Yarnall*/BethSF	5 Dec 42	30 Dec 43	590 *Paul Hamilton*/CharNY	20 Jan 43	25 Oct 43
544 *Boyd*/BethSP	2 Apr 42	8 May 43	591 *Twiggs*/CharNY	20 Jan 43	4 Nov 43
545 *Bradford*/BethSP	28 Apr 42	12 Jun 43	592 *Howorth*/PSNY	26 Nov 41	3 Apr 44
546 *Brown*/BethSP	27 Jun 42	10 Jul 43	593 *Killen*/PSNY	26 Nov 41	4 May 44
547 *Cowell*/BethSP	7 Sep 42	23 Aug 43	594 *Hart*/PSNY	10 Aug 43	4 Nov 44
550 *Capps*/Gulf	12 Jun 41	23 Jun 43	595 *Metcalfe*/PSNY	10 Aug 43	18 Nov 44
551 *David W. Taylor*/Gulf	12 Jun 41	18 Sep 43	596 *Shields*/PSNY	10 Aug 43	8 Feb 45
552 *Evans*/Gulf	21 Jul 41	11 Dec 43	597 *Wiley*/PSNY	10 Aug 43	22 Feb 45
553 *John D. Henley*/Gulf	21 Jul 41	2 Feb 44	629 *Abbot*/Bath	21 Sep 42	23 Apr 43
554 *Franks*/SeaTac	8 Aug 42	30 Jul 43	630 *Braine*/Bath	12 Oct 42	23 Apr 43
555 *Haggard*/SeaTac	27 Mar 42	31 Aug 43	631 *Erben*/Bath	28 Oct 42	28 May 43
556 *Hailey*/SeaTac	11 Apr 42	30 Sep 43	642 *Hale*/Bath	23 Nov 42	15 Jun 43
557 *Johnston*/SeaTac	6 May 42	27 Oct 43	643 *Sigourney*/Bath	7 Dec 42	29 Jun 43
558 *Laws*/SeaTac	19 May 42	18 Nov 43	644 *Stembel*/Bath	21 Dec 42	16 Jul 43
559 *Longshaw*/SeaTac	16 Jun 42	4 Dec 43	649 *Albert W. Grant*/CharNY	30 Dec 42	24 Nov 43
560 *Morrison*/SeaTac	30 Jun 42	18 Dec 43	650 *Caperton*/Bath	11 Jan 43	30 Jul 43
561 *Prichett*/SeaTac	20 Jul 42	15 Jan 44	651 *Cogswell*/Bath	1 Feb 43	17 Aug 43
562 *Robinson*/SeaTac	12 Aug 42	31 Jan 44	652 *Ingersoll*/Bath	18 Feb 43	31 Aug 43
563 *Ross*/SeaTac	7 Sep 42	21 Feb 44	653 *Knapp*/Bath	8 Mar 43	10 Jul 43
564 *Rowe*/SeaTac	7 Dec 42	13 Mar 44	654 *Bearss*/Gulf	14 Jul 42	25 Jul 43
565 *Smalley*/SeaTac	9 Feb 43	31 Mar 44	655 *John Hood*/Gulf	12 Oct 42	7 Jun 44
566 *Stoddard*/SeaTac	10 Mar 43	15 Apr 44	656 *Van Valkenburgh*/Gulf	15 Nov 42	2 Aug 44
567 *Watts*/SeaTac	26 Mar 43	29 Apr 44	657 *Charles J. Badger*/BethSI	24 Sep 42	23 Jul 43
568 *Wren*/SeaTac	24 Apr 43	29 Jan 44	658 *Colahan*/BethSI	24 Oct 42	23 Aug 43
569 *Aulick*/Orange	14 May 41	27 Oct 42	659 *Dashiell*/Fed	1 Oct 42	20 Mar 43
570 *Charles Ausburne*/Orange	14 May 41	24 Nov 42	660 *Bullard*/Fed	16 Oct 42	9 Apr 43
571 *Claxton*/Orange	25 Jun 41	8 Dec 42	661 *Kidd*/Fed	16 Oct 42	23 Apr 43
572 *Dyson*/Orange	25 Jun 41	30 Dec 42	662 *Bennion*/BosNY	19 Mar 43	14 Dec 43
573 *Harrison*/Orange	25 Jul 41	25 Jan 43	663 *Heywood L. Edwards*/BosNY	4 Jul 43	26 Jan 44
574 *John Rodgers*/Orange	25 Jul 41	9 Feb 43	664 *Richard P. Leary*/BosNY	4 Jul 43	23 Feb 44
575 *McKee*/Orange	2 Mar 42	31 Mar 43	665 *Bryant*/CharNY	30 Dec 42	4 Dec 43
576 *Murray*/Orange	16 Mar 42	20 Apr 43	666 *Black*/Fed	14 Nov 42	21 May 43
577 *Sproston*/Orange	1 Apr 42	19 May 43	667 *Chauncey*/Fed	14 Nov 42	31 May 43

Name/Builder	Laid Down	Commissioned
668 *Clarence K. Bronson*/Fed	9 Dec 42	11 Jun 43
669 *Cotten*/Fed	8 Feb 43	24 Jul 43
670 *Dortch*/Fed	2 Mar 43	7 Aug 43
671 *Gatling*/Fed	3 Mar 43	19 Aug 43
672 *Healy*/Fed	4 Mar 43	3 Sep 43
673 *Hickox*/Fed	12 Mar 43	10 Sep 43
674 *Hunt*/Fed	31 Mar 43	22 Sep 43
675 *Lewis Hancock*/Fed	31 Mar 43	29 Sep 43
676 *Marshall*/Fed	19 Apr 43	16 Oct 43
677 *McDermut*/Fed	14 Jun 43	19 Nov 43
678 *McGowan*/Fed	30 Jun 43	20 Dec 43
679 *McNair*/Fed	30 Jun 43	30 Dec 43
680 *Melvin*/Fed	6 Jul 43	24 Nov 43
681 *Hopewell*/BethSP	29 Oct 42	30 Sep 43
682 *Porterfield*/BethSP	12 Dec 42	30 Oct 43
683 *Stockham*/BethSF	19 Dec 42	11 Feb 44
684 *Wedderburn*/BethSF	10 Jan 43	9 Mar 44
685 *Picking*/BethSI	24 Nov 42	21 Sep 43
686 *Halsey Powell*/BethSI	4 Feb 43	25 Oct 43
687 *Uhlmann*/BethSI	6 Mar 43	22 Nov 43
688 *Remey*/Bath	22 Mar 43	30 Sep 43
689 *Wadleigh*/Bath	5 Apr 43	19 Oct 43
690 *Norman Scott*/Bath	26 Apr 43	5 Nov 43
691 *Mertz*/Bath	10 May 43	19 Nov 43
792 *Callaghan*/BethSP	21 Feb 43	27 Nov 43
793 *Cassin Young*/BethSP	18 Mar 43	31 Dec 43
794 *Irwin*/BethSP	2 May 43	14 Feb 44
795 *Preston*/BethSP	13 Jun 43	20 Mar 44
796 *Benham*/BethSI	3 Apr 43	20 Dec 43
797 *Cushing*/BethSI	3 May 43	17 Jan 44
798 *Monssen*/BethSI	1 Jun 43	14 Feb 44
799 *Jarvis*/SeaTac	7 Jun 43	3 Jun 44
800 *Porter*/SeaTac	6 Jul 43	24 Jun 44
801 *Colhoun*/SeaTac	3 Aug 43	8 Jul 44
802 *Gregory*/SeaTac	31 Aug 43	29 Jul 44
803 *Little*/SeaTac	13 Sep 43	19 Aug 44
804 *Rooks*/SeaTac	27 Oct 43	2 Sep 44